PLANTSMAN'S PROGRESS

Also by Alan Bloom

PRELUDE TO BRESSINGHAM

PLANTSMAN'S PROGRESS

by

ALAN BLOOM

TERENCE DALTON LIMITED
LAVENHAM   SUFFOLK
1976

published by

TERENCE DALTON LIMITED

ISBN 0 900963 67 0

Printed in 11/12 pt Baskerville Typeface

printed in Great Britain at

THE LAVENHAM PRESS LIMITED

LAVENHAM   SUFFOLK

Contents

Index of Illustrations

To Bridget, Robert and Adrian.

Aerial view showing Bressingham Hall with farm buildings in the centre. The Steam Museum is the large building with the white roof. Beyond are nursery fields and the big pond. The garden, with island beds amongst the trees, is bottom left.

Michael Warren

CHAPTER ONE

Aconite, Alpine . . . .

AS A Festival, Christmas is said to have its origins long before Anno Domini was used to register the years. Then it was entirely pagan, and has in fact become so again to the majority of people. In Before Christ times it undoubtedly had strong connections with the winter solstice, as the period between the end of one growing season, and the beginning of another. And although weather and temperature are as always the factors which control renewed growth, it is the garden lovers who watch for signs of it, once Christmas is over, regardless of whatever else the season means, festive or otherwise. Although growth and daylight are at their lowest ebb, and damp, cold weather offers little inducement, I am amongst those who cannot resist searching for signs of spring and renewed growth once Christmas is over. A New Year is only a day or two away, and one can usually find something to bring hope, if not cheer. And I find that the older I grow, the more of a miracle there is to be seen in the signs of another spring.

The lowly winter Aconite is scarcely a harbinger of spring, knowing that when its flowers have faded there can still come a belated wintry spell. But it is a New Year herald — the first in the succession of spring flowers from corms or bulbs, which ends with the tulips. Those who grow winter-flowering shrubs may well be cheered far more by seeing these and Erica *carnea* braving the weather, than by winter aconites and the rest. But as a specialist in hardy perennials I have a very soft spot for the range of Adonis, the first of which opens in January, almost regardless of wintry weather. This is a Japanese hybrid named 'Fukujakai'. Unless locked in by frost, its fat, coppery-green nubs will be through the soil at Christmas to reveal a hint of yellow in the tips. Within a week or two these will be opening at four to six inches high to reveal a glistening yellow flower three or four times the size of winter aconites. The joy it brings can be experienced indoors too. A week before last Christmas I lifted and potted two plants. In the conservatory they opened within days, and made a brilliant display with about twenty flowers on each plant. Outdoors it lasts till well after the next Adonis opens, and as its flowers fade to green the ferny foliage makes a pleasing mound. A. *amurensis* comes next, but the one in cultivation is double. I have never seen the single, but I rather think A. 'Fukujukai' has this as a parent. A *amurensis* 'plena' is a trifle dwarfer, and the flowers are even larger; again with a tinge of green in the gleaming, canary yellow. This will be in flower from early March to late April, with its low canopy of lacy, dark green fronds; by which time A. *volgensis* is showing strongly above ground. This makes a delicate, filigreed bushlet a foot or so tall, and is set with charming, single, buttercup-yellow flowers. Not far behind comes A. *vernalis,* which where happy will compel one to pause and gaze at its sheer beauty of form, erectly bushy with deep green filigree, carrying 1½-inch flowers of glistening yellow. All four Adonis prefer an open soil, not specially rich, but well drained. They have brownish, fibrous roots from a fleshy stock, not difficult to divide when dormant because new crowns are formed by the time the flowers have faded. The first two become dormant before midsummer, but A. *volgensis* keeps its greenery longer, and A. *vernalis* almost until autumn. Early autumn is of course the best time for planting and dividing.

It would be easier to ramble on about plants on a seasonal basis, but one reason for tackling this book alphabetically is that asides and anecdotes come to mind more readily letter by letter. My introduction to the realms of Alpines for instance, came just after I left school in 1922. I left, by the way, prematurely, simply because I wanted to work with plants. My father had just embarked full time on market growing at Oakington, five miles from Cambridge, and my urge to work outdoors fitted his need for a helper. With the rashness of youth I spent my first five shillings on purchasing a hundred alpines in twenty different kinds. In those days too there were firms who had large display advertisements for nursery stock at very low prices.

Aconitum 'Bressingham Spire'
raised by the author.

My father once asked a Mr Letts, who at that time was head of one such firm, how he made it pay. The answer came pat, but in a confidential whisper; "Because there's a fool born every minute." It was Edmunds & Co., of Milton, whose full-page advertisements in the *Horticultural Trade Journal* caught my eye, and to whom my valued order was given. At the bottom of the page was a list of about thirty kinds of alpines raised from seed; all at five shillings per hundred. I couldn't go wrong, even though five shillings was half a week's wages for a lad of my age. My selection included mixed Aubretia, Dianthus, Crucianella, Tunica and others, and as they were seedlings well under a year old I potted them into 3-inch pots, telling my parents that this was the beginning of my career as a producer of alpines.

In the same year I bought packets of seed of many other kinds from Thompson and Morgan, who then, as now, offered a wider range than any other firm. They cost twopence, threepence or fourpence a packet, and by the end of the year the fifty per cent or so kinds that grew were also ready for potting. But alas I was trying to run before I could walk, and it was decided I should leave home to gain more experience. I wince as memory tells me how brash and opinionated I must have been as a teenager. Having previously spent ten weeks at a Wisbech nursery immediately after leaving school in July, 1922, I came home determined to stay. It had been an unpleasant and unrewarding experience, but when my parents arranged for me to go to Wallace's at Tunbridge Wells, a year later, I raised no real objection. A small voice inside told me I did not know so much about plants as I had been imagining, and that to achieve the lively ambitions I held—as well as the craving for status; to be released from the necessity of being told what to do—then I'd best give in.

At Wallace's I became "crock-boy" at fifteen shillings a week of fifty-two hours. It was my job to wash and crock pots, ready for a superior to use them for potting alpines; and to sift and barrow the soil for mixing with sand and leafmould as directed. With the aid of another boy, two hundred six-feet by four-feet pitlights had to be taken off the alpine frames each morning for the five or six months of winter, and replaced every evening. There were no short-cuts and no skimping allowed for any of these tasks. After eight months, believing I was worthy of a better job at more money, I applied to John Charlton, partner in Arthur Charlton and Sons, and it so happened they needed someone to take charge of their small alpine department of about 40,000 plants. I was eighteen, and the jump to thirty shillings a week not only made me self-supporting, but made me more big-headed than ever. How John Charlton found the patience to put up with some of the mistakes I made I'll never know. But he did, and in later years always made me welcome when I visited him. His range of plants was not very wide, but it included all what he termed "the bread-and-butter kinds". I persuaded him to enlarge it, and again attempted to raise a number of fresh kinds, new to me also, from Thompson and Morgan's seeds.

I was also asked to propagate some of the herbaceous subjects. These grew in a long, narrow strip of land bounded on one side by the L.B.S.C. Railway embankment, and on the other by a large ditch. Amongst the perennials to be propagated was a collection of Phlox which John Charlton had purchased in situ on an allotment. I believed Tommy Carlile, then blossoming out as a specialist nurseryman at Twyford, with a catalogue headed "Carlile's Thousand & One Best Plants", had suggested a propagating method which obviated the risk of eelworm, to which plants from tip cuttings were prone. The method was to use a carving knife, and with it gouge out the central rootstock, leaving only the fibrous roots in the ground, and filling up the hole so made with sand. The task beat me. My hands blistered, and finally the carving knife snapped before a quarter were done, so hardy and woody were those old plants of Phlox.

I'd been at Charlton's nearly a year by this time, and my first love was still for alpines. Though my request for a rise in wages put me half-a-crown a week better off, I decided to move, and advertised myself in the *Horticultural Trade Journal*. There were three replies. I fancied going north, and so turned down Stewart's of Wimborne. And because Gayborder Nurseries were not so far north as Longster's of Malton, I accepted the challenge offered by Mr Longster to work up an alpines department because he also offered more money, at two pounds per week. There a glasshouse for seed raising and propagating was placed at my disposal, and again Thompson and Morgan's seed were to be the beginnings of the new department. But promises of plant stock, pots and a plunge bed site were not kept as quickly as I'd been led to believe. From the start I was put onto jobs unconnected with the one I'd applied for. Perhaps Mr Longster too was having second thoughts about my abilities, for he stone-walled my pleas and complaints, However, he invited me to take charge of a market stall at York on Saturdays, but when this met with poor results I decided Malton was no place for me.

The name R. V. Roger was being quoted by Longster's men. They said he was a go-ahead nurseryman, and I decided to bike over the eight miles to Pickering one evening. Yes, he would take me on as propagator under his foreman, Sid Fasoms, and after only six weeks at Malton I moved on. R. V. Roger, a handsome bachelor, (at that time), six foot three tall, was certainly go-ahead, and had a reputation for quality trees and shrubs, with herbaceous and alpines also flourishing, but taking second place. There I learned with admiration how one man's drive could inspire his helpers, and he encouraged me to set targets for output. Discipline was fairly strict, but I came to resent Sid Fasoms' interference, which I considered uncalled-for. I preferred to think of Mr Roger and not Sid as my superior and boss.

Sid had been a gardener with Reginald Farrer until the latter's early death, and was inclined to trade on this distinction. He had two of the three small glasshouses under his special care, and the other, for propagating, I considered was under mine. No doubt he had the right to find fault with what I did, but it was this

I resented. Although at the time he was over forty, and I was under twenty, he once criticised something I was doing in my greenhouse and it made me boil over. I ordered him out, and slowly advanced with pointing finger, as he tried first to assert his authority. But slowly he backed away. My sense of complete victory was short-lived, for within an hour Mr Roger was lecturing me on the need to keep the peace. It was a lecture rather than the severe reprimand I might have expected, but the effect was salutary on both parties. Sid too must have been lectured—or asked to humour me—for he never interfered again, and for the rest of the time I stayed at Pickering we were on good terms. I loved Pickering and the moors beyond, and made friends, although I stayed there less than a year. It was good to go back, as I did several times over the next forty years, and be welcomed not least by R. V. Roger, who having worked up the finest nursery in Yorkshire, died as a result of a car accident soon after his two sons had taken over.

It was during my stay there that two other opportunities for experience—apart from learning about plants—came my way. I was given the very pleasant task of making a small rock-garden for a customer at Goathland, and of staging exhibits at York Gala Flower Show and Roundhay Park Show, just outside Leeds. However, both kindled ambitions that were to prove dead-ends in later years.

Back home at Oakington, early in 1926, I believed I possessed all that was needed by way of knowledge and experience to forge ahead. There had been a period whilst at Pickering when I fancied my future lay more on the academic side—to go to a Botanic Garden, with the ultimate aim of becoming a plant hunter. Kingdon-Ward's and Farrer's books on their expeditions had inspired this, but in the end the ambition to be a plant producer—a master nurseryman—topped the scales. There were fifteen acres of good land at Oakington, and since I was the only one of three brothers keen on horticulture my father was willing enough to let me go in for plants; so long as I helped with his market growing of fruit and flowers. The one ingredient lacking was capital, and so Father matched my savings from wages of about five pounds with a similar amount; to be spent mainly on stock plants of alpines and more packets of seeds.

The nearest established nursery for alpines was Casburn and Welch, just outside Cambridge, and in twos, fours and sixes of a kind a selection was made. Money was very tight indeed, but believing a rock-garden on which to grow stock plants was important, this became the next priority. A ton of cheap stone wasn't much of an outlay, and the result of trying to imitate a piece of natural outcropping wasn't very pleasing, but at least the plants grew well, and provided cuttings, divisions and seed. During that summer, when the General Strike ended just in time to avoid disaster to Father's market flower crops, most of my time had to be spent in cutting, bunching and packing Pyrethrums, Gypsophila and Statice and the rest, but slowly stocks of alpines in pots increased. So did my enthusiasm, even if there was scarcely anything yet to sell.

Amongst the choicer kinds I'd bought was Asperula *suberosa*. It grew well, and by pulling its delicate roots, each with a tiny grey shoot, to pieces in early spring, the four original plants made over thirty, and would divide again within a year to make enough to sell. Its tiny, shell-pink flowers on grey, woolly tufts only two inches high were fascinatingly beautiful to me, and made me spurn the Crucianella *stylosa*. which also had heads of pink flowers, because it was not only rank and invasive, but it stank. This, left over from my first attempt to grow seedling alpines, or the twenty varieties bought for five shillings, held very little appeal now that I was on to choice subjects. These included such treasures as Campanulas 'R. B. Loder' and 'Warleyense', some Kabschia *saxifragas*, Hypericum *coris*, and others I'd fallen for without much thought for demand when I had enough to sell. Looking back, I can see this as probably a characteristic failing — of justifying what I wanted to do or grow by kidding myself it would pay off. Sometimes it did, and if quite often it didn't it was at least enjoyable until proof of wrong judgement came.

In one sense I suppose I have always been a dabbler. I still find the lure of plants irresistible; wanting to try out anything that might have some decorative value in alpines or the taller perennials — between which I see no strict dividing line. In practice any difference must lie in a plant's adaptability to a given soil, site or situation. One example comes to mind, of a plant I'd grown for three years, and was inclined to throw out as worthless, because it failed to flower. Amongst some subjects new to me from Frikart's nursery, in Switzerland, was an Achillea. It grew quite quickly but rather untidily, with heads of yellow, eighteen inches tall. Not far away , in my garden, was growing A. *clypeolata*, also yellow-headed and with quite' pretty, silvery foliage — which chaffinches plucked at nesting time. Seedlings raised from the new Swiss variety — I forget its name — showed variations. I selected two, both of which I thought were improvements, and in deciding to propagate them come spring, dubbed the pale yellow one 'Moonshine', and the deeper one 'Sunshine'. Both had died out when spring arrived; as had most of the score or so seedlings. One that survived produced abundant silvery foliage but no flowers, and I left it where it was, in the partial shade of an apple tree, just in case it flowered the following year. But it didn't flower that year or the next, though it grew into a large plant. Then, having a group space empty in the garden, and not knowing what to fill it with, I dug up the clump of Achillea and split it into nine or ten, but with little hope that it would do more than act as a ground coverer. Its position was in full sun, and the soil poor and stoney, but it flowered, with wide heads of bright lemon yellow, both that year and the next. By that time, realizing it was distinctive and reliable — and how nearly I'd slipped up — I gave it the name 'Moonshine' in memory of the one by that name which had not survived. As a Cinderella it not only gained an Award of Merit from the R.H.S., but in the following years our average sales annually have been somewhere between three and five thousand plants, and it is in practically every hardy plant nurseryman's catalogue, both in Britain and overseas. Sometimes dabbling pays — if only to offset loss from growing kinds which do not take on.

CHAPTER TWO

Bloom, Bergenia . . . .

BLOOM is an appropriate name for a grower of flowers, but Reany's book gives its origin as "a worker in iron". Apart from my father, none of my forebears, as far as I've been able to trace, were either iron workers or professionals in horticulture. As far back as 1700 they were East Anglian yeomen or merchants. But my father broke away from the shopkeeping into which his tyrannical parent had forced him. He had grown flowers for market as a sideline since 1900, longing for the day when he could sell the shop and grow fruit and flowers full time. That time did not come till 1922 when, having turned fifty, he moved from the stiff clay at Over to the easier working soil at Oakington. In both places he gained the reputation of being a glutton for work, and if only his slogging had been matched by reward he would have retired a wealthy man. As it was, he had to live frugally all his life, and his love of work kept him active, (in spite of life-long digestive troubles), till he was eighty-six. It was overstrain—from cutting down an over-grown hedge—that brought his life to an end.

His love of flowers was unbounded, and one of his few relaxations was to paint them—even when he was over eighty. Having had no horticultural training he had to feel his way—or follow his fancy—in what he grew, with something of the Micawber optimism. But so often crops did not come up to expectations; or if they did then it would be a heat-wave or some other cause for a glutted market and low prices. The bustle of a shed full of cut flowers being packed for Birmingham, Manchester, Sheffield or Covent Garden is an indelible childhood memory for me. And so is father's face at breakfast time, when, having already done two or three hours' flower-cutting, he opened the returns from the market salesmen.

"Half-a-crown a box doesn't pay for the cutting and carriage," was often his bitter complaint. But enough at other periods did pay sufficiently to keep him going. One never knew in advance what flowers would fetch, and maybe it was the element of gambling that was the spice for him. It was a gamble that prompted him, about 1910, to go in for making jam to sell to grocers, as another sideline. After the first year or two he increased production, and another of my earliest memories is the smell and sight of hundreds of full jam-jars piled up on benches. One day there was a horrid crashing noise and some shrieks. Father emerged from the shed, the picture of dejection, for a bench carrying two tons of jam that was being sealed down had collapsed. The loss nearly broke him, and he never made any more.

Back with flowers and fruit, with its ups and downs, I became sufficiently involved to feel the conflicts and traumas which market growing engenders. The element of chance is so strong that it has its parallels with horse-racing. Form is studied in previous market or cropping performance; the going is indicated by weather factors, and the results, winners or losers, in the sale returns from various markets. There was a winner in 1928 with the double white button Pyrethrum *parthenium*. We dubbed it "Stinker" because of its astringent odour, but it was easy to cut, bunch and pack, and for two weeks fifty or sixty boxes were sent off daily to Birmingham, averaging about seven shillings a box clear—which was a good price for what it was. But in doubling the quantities grown in 1929, from autumn rooted cuttings, the dry summer did not suit it, and the returns were less than half.

It was in 1929 that from divisions of a single plant selected from some seedling Heucheras, raised in 1923, the stock had been increased to a bed covering half an acre. As an improvement on H. *brizoides* 'gracillima' it had already sold well in small lots at Covent Garden, and now, we believed, was the time for full rewards. It was going to be a certain winner. But though the first few boxes fetched an exciting pound a box, something went wrong. Monro's, the salesmen, took exception to an aspersion Father had made in a letter; that the flowers in some other consignment had been mishandled by them. They reckoned it was slight on their integrity, and they flatly refused to take any more flowers from us. Heuchera 'Bloom's Variety' had, therefore, to be sent to other salesmen at several different markets, but none returned prices anywhere near that made by Monro's. And it was such a tedious

Heuchera 'Bressingham' hybrids.

Dianthus 'Oakington' hybrid in the front of the border. This was raised by the author in 1931.

subject to cut and bunch that in the end most of the half-acre bed had to be destroyed. As a decorative plant it was the first subject my father had raised to be given an Award of Merit by the R.H.S., and it was featured on the first Chelsea exhibit we put up, in 1931.

By this time Father had left Oakington to take over a derelict glasshouse nursery at Mildenhall. At twenty-four I was my own master, recently married to a florist. In spite of the Depression and the scarcity of cash, my plant-growing department could now expand, and steadily oust the market gardening. Though grateful to my parents for moving out, my own ambitions were paramount just then. I saw the move as being a family arrangement to accommodate my younger brother, who wished to join Father at Mildenhall, since both had a special liking for glasshouse crops, and I preferred an outdoor nursery. And it was to be a real nursery, not a market garden, though in the four years I'd been at Oakington what modest development there had been was in sales of plants to the trade, rather than direct retail. Several distant shows at which I'd exhibited both alpines and perennials had scarcely paid. There were at that time too many exhibiting nurserymen — mostly well-established firms — seeking the few orders there were to be had. I also had a stall for several weeks each year on local markets — Cambridge, St Ives, Ely and Newmarket — but these didn't bring in much either. Five pounds in sales was reckoned to be quite good, but often takings were much less. I spent my twenty-first birthday on a Cambridge Saturday Market stall, and brought home twenty-eight shillings. The total sales turnover for plants, flowers, fruit and seeds for 1929 was £572, with a net profit of £149.

Being used to the frugality that perennial shortage of money imposes, I suppose the optimism I held on taking over the Oakington nursery in 1931 had some foundation. Things could scarcely get worse. Having now given up market stalls and hawking plants round the residential districts of Cambridge — both of which I loathed — my ambitions centred on growing plants for the trade; selling through a catalogue and by advertising in the *Horticultural Trade Journal*. My first Trade List which I knocked out four copies at a time on a £2 typewriter, offered forty-eight kinds of plants; and fifty-six copies were posted to retailing nurserymen. That was in autumn, 1926, but for the next four years lists — growing in size — were run off on a Gestetner. By 1931 there were four hundred items to offer, and because we had been allocated a small table space at Chelsea that year a retail catalogue was also issued. But retail selling had less and less appeal for me. The pull was all for growing plants, for I was a poor salesman. I begrudged the time spent standing for hours beside an exhibit waiting to book orders, and answering questions which seldom led to orders, when I might have been propagating, potting or planting.

Some people asked if Bloom was just a trading name — and even this annoyed me when my explanations brought some fatuous comment. In the four years previous to 1931 it had been C. H. Bloom and Son, but it was when I changed it to Bloom's Nurseries that people at shows queried it. A trifling matter maybe, but it was just one of the weights that piled up, and persuaded me that my future as a nurseryman lay in wholesale production. By 1934 I was wholesale only, for by that time plants for sale had completely ousted those grown for market. By 1939 there were thirty-six acres under plants, including 150,000 alpines in pots, and the catalogue, now properly printed, listed 1,872 species and varieties of plants, which thirty-six helpers and I had produced.

The basic wholesale price of plants, for several years up to 1939, had been twenty-five shillings per hundred. A few, such as Nepeta *mussinii,* were only twenty shillings. Orders were carriage paid for cash with order over two pounds. Rail deliveries were excellent by modern standards, and Oakington station was only a few hundred yards distant, where market growers were still loading boxes of flowers and sieves of fruit. I pitied them, for I'd found a better way of life on the land than either them or the farmers.

I believed my three rules of business were paying off. They were; to sell only the best possible quality plants, at reasonable prices and to give prompt despatch with careful packing. For ten years I'd observed those rules, and I was no longer poor. I'd even bought a two hundred acre farm in the Fens, with ideas of competing with the Dutchmen who were still shipping vast quantities of plants as well as bulbs to Britain at lower prices, because their labour was cheaper than ours.

Those pre-war years were both exciting and exacting for me. My ambitions expanded with success, and tended to blank off any leanings I had for growing plants purely for decorative effect. I loved plants, none the less, and it was a joy to see them flower from start to finish without having to cut them as they neared perfection, to be sent off to distant markets. Plant production and cut flower production were, I believed, incompatible, and to a large extent I also believed decorative gardening was for me incompatible with the business of being a proper nurseryman. For me, a plant's value during that period lay more in its commercial possibilities, and my aesthetic senses were satisfied in having a wide variety in pots, or in rows in the fields adjoining Meadow House, in which my family and I lived. There were several kinds that refused to grow in the alkaline soil at Oakington. I tried a good many, but even the liberal use of peat was defeated by the lime in the water. It was more interesting and rewarding to go in for breeding new varieties, or to purchase novelties from other raisers and work up stocks to sell as quickly as possible.

Looking through my pre-war catalogues, some subjects now quite important were not grown at all then. Bergenias are amongst those missing altogether. They were known as Megaseas then, and though one occasionally saw them in out-of-the-way places in a garden, they were spurned in a general way, as being not worth growing by self-respecting gardeners or by nurserymen. Their present popularity is not due, as with some plants, to changes of fashion, but rather to economic and social factors. In the thirties far more people employed gardeners, though in total there were far fewer houses with gardens. The well-to-do with sizeable gardens had their conventional beds, shrubberies and herbaceous borders, and Bergenias were much too ordinary, too coarse and invasive to be included in the latter. If grown at all Bergenia would be in some dark or shady corner, where little else but London Pride, Periwinkle or Foxgloves would survive. And the paid gardener would concentrate on bedding out, keeping the borders trimmed, staked and stocked with Delphiniums, Lupins, Iris and Michaelmas Daisies, which were then at their zenith of popularity, despite the chores they involved.

Post-war gardening was forced into a different channel. The emphasis came down inexorably on labour-saving, and a good many herbaceous borders had become a chaos of weeds and the most persistent perennials, which had themselves become weedy. Those beyond redemption or restoration gave way to shrub borders, and where annual bedding had been possible and desirable before wartime austerities began, these too came in for shrubs or grass. It was an era of transition. Labour-saving began as a necessity, and from necessity there emerged a new term for a range of plants that would fill spaces, either between shrubs or anywhere else, if the owner wished to have done with traditional or conventional labour-demanding beds. The term was "Ground Cover Plants". Unlike "Herbaceous Border", which meant something different for different individuals, or the over-simple "Bedding

A field of Delphiniums at Bressingham, circa 1954.

Out", or the inadequate, inaccurate "Rockery", "Ground Cover" stood baldly for what it said — plants which covered the ground with little or no subsequent attention. With such plants foliage, along with weed-smothering ability, counted far more as virtues than the flowers they produced, and if the effect was relatively dull, the fact that they eliminated work was all that mattered.

It was the horticultural scribes who did most to popularise the range of ground cover plants. But it was such practical gardeners as Margery Fish who did the pioneering work. Subjects like Bergenias, Lamiums, Vincas, Hypericum *calycinum* and several more were not exactly languishing, but had merely been relegated to out-of-the-way places, until the pioneers saw there was now a need to be filled.

In making her garden at Lambrook Manor, Margery Fish stocked it with out-of-the-ordinary kinds as well as accepted favourites. She followed no conventional rules, but always experimented; trying out the unfamiliar, and studying plant behaviour under varying conditions. The overall effect was one of gardening exuberance, and in her writings she was able to recommend unusual kinds to suit the demand for trouble-freedom. Beneath her sometimes forbidding manner there was a very warm heart. It responded to anyone in whom she found a love of plants; not merely those that made a colourful display, but for form and grace, even if this existed in foliage alone. It was a privilege to know her; to give and be given hospitality, and to swap both plants and cultivating experiences with her. The vogue for grey, silver and variegated-leaved plants was largely prompted by Margery Fish, and her Artemisia 'Lambrook Silver' is still much in demand. Bergenia 'Margery Fish' was one of several raised by Mr Pugsley of Derby. He named it posthumously in her honour, for the contributions she made to present-day gardening with hardy plants, and I fancy as time goes on she will rank with those other women stalwarts of an earlier age; Gertrude Jekyll and Ellen Willmott.

Lupin 'Bressingham Sunshine'.

I have yet to find a place where Bergenias will not grow—sun or shade, moist or dry, no matter what the soil may be. Their spread is only on the surface, and if chopped back their chunky, ground-hugging growths, from which the shiny, cabbagy, deep green leaves come, will very soon sprout with new rosettes, and no weeds will live for long under their canopy. Being surface-rooting they respond to top dressings of soil in spring, just before the buds appear, and this is worth-while, especially with the brighter-flowered varieties, like 'Ballawley', 'Abendglut', and 'Margery Fish'.

Not much can be said in this book about shrubs, for I know relatively little about them. One that comes to mind, beginning with B, is worth a mention, because so many visitors have seen it in my garden asked its name—Bupleurum *fruticosum*. I raised some seedlings years ago, to help fill a space where shrubs were called for. Its habit is bushy, and the slightly blue-green, oval leaves are evergreen. Its little heads of sulphur-yellow flowers continue for many weeks when most flowering shrubs have finished. With me it reaches six feet or so, more or less taking care of itself without attention, beyond a very occasional pruning to encourage shapeliness. All it needs is a sunny position, and as mine is in a dry place, it can be said to be drought-resistant and long-lived.

Berberis *lolodgensis* appealed more to me than any other amongst a collection of about a dozen kinds I acquired at the same time, and for the same purpose. Its clusters of rich, orange flowers made a fine show for several years against a background of conifers, but having neglected to prune it, so as to encourage new basal growth, it began to languish. Or it may have been the soil, which was sticky and rather poorly drained, and now, rather belatedly, I've taken some cuttings in the hope of getting it going again.

CHAPTER THREE

Celandine, Campanula . . . .

CELANDINES, Buttercups and most Calthas have more than family relationships in common. Yellow is their basic colour; but it is the glistening sheen they have that appeals to me so much. Celandines are in fact my favourite weeds, and if they are growing harmlessly I leave them alone, because of the cheerful display they make in spring. In any case, their little clustered bulblets lie dormant for eight months of the year, and can scarcely be harmful to other plants. This long period of complete dormancy has been a drawback to my growing variations of both the Greater and the Lesser Celandine, which incidentally are botanically unrelated, going under the names of Chelidonium *majus* (Papaveraceae), and Ranunculus *ficaria*. Some are quite pretty, but they inevitably leave a bare patch after June, unless grown in company with something else for ground cover.

Calthas need nothing for company. All they need is moisture, but though as Kingcups or Marsh Marigolds they are mostly classified as "marginal" subjects, most of them will grow quite well in soil which does not dry out. The single yellow native Caltha *palustris* is undoubtedly best beside water, where it will naturalize if given the chance. This is not necessarily so with the double, C. *palustris* 'plena', which will make a splendid show in any moist soil. At about nine inches tall it is less upright than the wild type, (of which I recently found a self-sown seedling growing 2½ feet tall, to grow under trial for comparison), but it is a more persistent perennial, easily divided after flowering, or in early autumn. As a garden subject I rate it very highly indeed. C. *polypetala* is tall, and will grow in anything from merely moist soil down to land submerged in as much as a foot of water, carrying large rounded leaves, and above these loose sprays of bright yellow flowers 1½ inches across, in April to May—later than C. *palustris*.

C. *tyermannii* is interesting. This too has large flowers of burnished golden yellow, but whilst the leaves are canopied above on twelve inch stalks, the flowering stems droop as they become branched, and in prostrating themselves will take root at the joints where they touch damp soil. This is the "Pope's Marigold"—so called because it came to light in the Vatican garden. It flowers in late spring and early summer.

The earliest to flower with me is the diminutive C. *sylvestris,* growing only three to four inches high, with deep yellow flowers, but it is inclined to sulk, resenting division and refusing to yield seed.

Caltha *palustris* — the Kingcup or Marsh Marigold in April.

Seed is sparse too with the lovely, pure white C. *leptosepala,* but at least it will increase slowly. This is a little charmer, no more than about eight inches high, flowering in April and May, and far more pleasing than what goes for C. *palustris* 'alba', which has off-white flowers three weeks to a month earlier than the other type. It is so different in growth and habit to the wild Kingcup that I'm inclined to believe it is a different species, though I've been too lazy to seek proof of this.

It was the very lean year of 1929 that made me realize that the need to make a living must come before a love for plants and the urge to collect a wide variety. The poor returns for that year could be blamed on a severe frost in February and March, followed by a long, droughty summer. I was not very fit, having overdone speed skating during the frost, bringing on yellow jaundice, which took a long time to clear up. But the fact was both my father and I, in our respective and sometimes conflicting spheres, were perhaps too much concerned with cultivating, and gave too little attention to what could be profitably sold. My mother had a better business head than either of us, but although she scraped and saved as best she could, she was at a disadvantage. All she could do was advise us to cut back and stick to what paid best to grow, but with my younger brother George coming to join in, after five years in the printing business, the contribution he made during 1930 did little more than offset the cost of his keep. But at least he relieved me of the chore of manning market stalls, which I loathed, and gave me time which I used for expanding the stock of alpines for sale.

It went against the grain for me to cut down on the number of kinds I grew, although there was no denying the need for restriction to what would sell. I had to grow what prospective customers liked, and leave my own preferences out of it. Over the previous three years I'd been collecting Campanulas because I liked them, and was rather proud of having 109, mostly species. But no more than twenty of these were at all in demand, and it hurt to have to reduce to about forty kinds. I hoped this number would be justified if sales of alpines increased generally, and in any case I'd raised some from seed, amongst which were some promising variations. Of the final selection of four which I subsequently named at least three are still in cultivation. Three were variations of C. *pusilla* (cochlearifolia); C. 'Oakington Blue', 'Cambridge Blue' and 'Blue Tit', and the fourth, C. *lactiflora* 'Pouffe', is still a good seller. Till it appeared, by sheer luck, C. *lactiflora* itself was never less than about three feet tall, with a loose head of light lavender-blue bells in June to July. There was also a white, but 'Pouffe' seemed to be a good name for mine, which made a wide mound of light green leaves, only nine inches high, decked with pale lavender bells from June to August, before dying back to a fleshy rootstock.

One of the fascinating features of the genus Campanula, of which there are about 250 species, is the vastly different habits of growth, from the creeping C. *pusillas,* with their dainty bells, only two or three inches high, or the rare and difficult C. *zoysii,* to the variations C. *lactiflora* or C. *latifolia,* some of which will attain six feet. The namesake of the variety C. *latiloba* 'Percy Piper' has been responsible for raising several plants since I came to Bressingham. He was here already as gardener and odd job man to the previous owners, but they were not garden-minded employers, and quite often Percy bought flower seeds out of his own pocket so as to brighten up the dull surroundings of the house. With some encouragement from me he "fiddled" as he termed it, with a camel hair brush, and together we would look over batches of resultant seedlings as they came into flower. Sometimes he followed his own theories and ideas as to what might yield a cross or improvement, and though not very systematic, preferring not to bother about keeping written records, he has come up with several successes. I liked the Campanula named after him, because it had more of the good and less of the bad qualities of both parents, C. *persicifolia* and C. *latiloba* (syn grandis). It makes spreading, evergreen rosettes, and sends up three-foot stems in June and July of rich, deep blue saucers.

More recently, the results of Percy's "fiddling" with Crocosmia proved to be very exciting. I suppose I was largely responsible for popularizing Crocosmia *masonorum,* which previously had suffered from the unwarranted stigman of not being hardy. The 1963 winter proved that it was, for it came through despite the soil at Bressingham being frozen iron hard to a depth of eighteen inches. From seed C. *masonorum* showed slight variations, and since it is closely allied both to Antholyza and Montbretia, (and Curtonus), we fancied it might yield crosses with these.

Antholyza *paniculata* was vigorous and very hardy, but with rather small flowers of a dull, deep orange colour, whereas most of the hybrid Montbretias were not fully hardy, though flowers were larger and more colourful.

Percy's unrecorded seedlings flowered after two years. There were several hundreds, planted in rows near my house, and from them over thirty were staked to grow on for further trial, the rest being dumped. After two more years each selection was lifted, and with corms having increased from two to ten each, it needed another two years of careful observation to reduce them to ten or twelve of the best. This was repeated till they came down to five or six, and then began the process of working up stocks, having named them 'Emberglow', 'Spitfire', 'Bressingham', 'Blaze', 'Mars' and 'Lucifer'. The latter was the tallest, at over three feet, and though sturdy in growth, like an Antholyza, with flowers far larger, on strong wiry stems, and sword-like leaves, and the colour a fiery deep oragne-scarlet, it increased but slowly. By the time we had two thousand of some of the others there were less than two hundred 'Lucifer'. In the others, finally selected, one could spot the dominant parentage; some leaning towards Crocosmia, others to Montbretia. But all were very showy indeed during the July to August period, with heights varying from barely two feet to about three feet, and colours from orange to flame red — and everyone fell for them

I have no intention of relegating Crocosmia *masonorum* because of these new varieties, for it remains a very good garden plant. One of its outstanding features, which 'Lucifer' also possesses, is the way in which the terminal flower spray arches over to make the trumpet shaped flowers face upwards — rather like a smaller Hemerocallis in shape. Montbretias are more inclined to open obliquely sideways on less open sprays. Some Montbretia species are weedy because of their rapid spread, and should be discarded in favour of better kinds. Those with Antholyza or Crocosmia blood make shoots below ground which become corms, and so increase, but new corms are made each year immediately above the old ones which have flowered. The lower corms should be left attached, because they appear to act as food storage. At any rate, when I once separated them, hoping thereby to increase the stock more quickly, very few of the lower old corms survived, and the younger, upper ones were shy to flower that year.

As a closely allied generic group, Antholyza, Crocosmia, Curtonus, Montbretia and Tritonia are in need of sorting out. No-one seems to know for sure which is which. Perhaps they are too difficult for any taxonymist to tackle with any certainty of success, or likelihood of acceptance by others. I placed our new crosses — quite arbitrarily — all under Crocosmia, because it would only compound the existing confusion to do otherwise. By some precepts those which are an obvious cross between Crocosmia and Antholyza should have been called "Crocolyza," to signify a bi-generic hybrid. But I couldn't bring myself to inflict such an ugly name on such a beautiful subject as 'Lucifer', which I would place very near the top if I were to list the new varieties I've raised and named in order of merit. They would make a list which would be somewhere between eighty and a hundred names long over the past forty-five years.

Crocosmias, by the way, ask for nothing more than just ordinary garden soil, and a sunny place, and are best planted in early spring. The flowers last well in water.

To drop back a generation, the year 1930 was not the only one in which I had to make a reassessment. Another came in 1934, when I decided to go wholesale only, and again in 1938, when I went in for farming as well. This was the subject of my first book, *The Farm in the Fen*. It led to my moving to Bressingham in 1946. But in 1948 an unsettled mind took me to Canada, and after nearly two years there sometimes on the breadline, I saw how foolish a venture it was, and returned to Bressingham to begin again, wiser but poorer. This story is told in *Prelude to Bressingham*, (Terence Dalton, 1975), but looking back on 1949, I see it as a barren year in more ways than one. The farm itself, in Southern Ontario, was pretty barren, but having to spend most of that blazing summer digging wells and trenches for water pipes to supply the home also made me pine for flowers and plants which were entirely absent. I'd imported a collection of Bressingham plants whilst still on Vancouver Island, but had to leave these before any came into flower. Those two years in Canada were tough, and I was very close to ruin by the time I decided to come home, chastened, but willing enough now to face the task of restoring the nursery business which I'd shirked. I'd taken a wrong turning, but had at least learned that escapism doesn't work, and once down to earth again, back came, almost overwhelmingly, the love of plants, not only because plants were my business, but because they were necessary as a background to life.

I had not realized, either, how closely linked one's roots are to one's chosen job, until I found Canadian soil was no good for transplanting mine into. Moving from Cambridgeshire to Norfolk scarcely disturbed them at all. The grim winter of 1947 had something to do with my decision to emigrate to Canada, but the main impulse was more personal and domestic. Some people never make roots, because they cannot find soil in which they can flourish.

Claire was one of these. She had university degrees, and had been on research work dealing with fruit and vegetables, but asked for a job to be in more direct contact with plants. Not long before, a very useful girl assistant for the garden had left after only a year, because of her infatuation for a married man more than old enough to be her father. I took Claire on gladly, for there was a good opening for someone intelligent and keen to learn about plants. It was autumn, and as winter came she pleaded for an inside job, because she felt the cold, though she was of strapping build. But she had neither the incentive nor the aptitude for work. Time and productivity meant nothing to her, and she'd make job—such as preparing

'The Dell', before being converted into garden, 1957.

cuttings or extracting seed — last all day, when it could have been done in an hour or two. She went from one type of job to another, with my patience running out as my hopes receded. Whether handling cuttings or seedlings, weeding or trimming it made no difference, and she confessed that her fingers were all thumbs on any such work. When spring came — the rush period, when she could have earned her pay, had she but grasped the most elementary skills — she gave up and left, still not knowing what, at twenty-eight, she wanted to do with her life.

View through doorway of flint garden shelter, built by author.

When I moved to Bressingham in October, 1946, one of my resolves was to change its two hundred acres from being what the estate agents termed a "Gentleman's Farm" into something much more productive. Much of it lay in a marshy valley bottom, and had been allowed to grow wild for the benefit of gentlemen with twelve-bore guns. One room in the house was in fact called the Gun Room — and still is, in spite of my having no gun. There was a dip of about an acre in the meadow in front of the house, called the Dell, and this I saw as a potential garden some day. But in 1946/7, apart from scrub clearance in the fenny valley bottom, my main concern was to move the remnants of stock from the Oakington nursery to Bressingham, and on to fields which had never before grown other than grass or farm crops. It could not have been a worse winter for such a move, especially as there were no suitable buildings for nursery work. We used hen huts for splitting plants, until the cold drove us out and into the house scullery. Losses due to flood and frost that winter were heavy, and a following drought took off even more precious plants — decimated already by wartime restrictions. In some cases there were only a dozen or so of a kind left as nucleus stock, and in the case of Centaurea *pulchra* 'major' there was only one, and a poor specimen at that. I planted it along with a few other remnants in the vegetable plot near the house, and it was still there when I returned from Canada three years later.

It was a challenge, or perhaps more correctly an example of what amounted to a much greater, more intricate challenge, to get my own roots down again where they really belonged; to work up stocks of the many choice subjects which had languished or vanished since 1939. To knife that one Centaurea, and make it into four or five was a beginning in the process. In two or three years' time those divisions would be large enough to cut up again, and eventually, by this means, some years later, there were several hundred, and at last it could be offered for sale. This aspect of a plantsman's life has always appealed to me, and the pleasure it gives me to work up a stock, no matter how long it takes, from one plant, by one means or another, comes as compensation for the inevitable failures and disappointments. Both must be the lot of all plantsmen.

Centaurea *pulchra* 'major' is still seldom to be seen in gardens, though it is such a handsome subject. Its roots go deeply, not to become a nuisance, like Acanthus and Oriental Poppies, but to make a stout clump that will remain trouble-free for years in any sunny place and well-drained soil. Its large, deeply-cut leaves are silvery-grey, and three-foot stems carry bright pink, tufty Cornflower heads in June to July.

Cautleya *robusta* is also rarely to be seen, but needs to be in fairly rich soil in either sun or shade, where it is not too dry. Its fleshy, clawlike roots increase below ground where happy, and stiffly erect stems have clasping, sheathed foliage, through which come spikes of deep orange, lipped flowers in late summer, after the style of a Canna or Hedichyum. The upper sections of the stems, (which reach 3½ feet), have a reddish hue. As a precaution against deep frost penetration I cover the group space with litter in winter, and though it grows for me in a neutral soil, with exotic abundance, I doubt if it would do so in drier, alkaline conditions.

CHAPTER FOUR

Desiderata, Dierama . . . .

DESIDERATA is a word I had no occasion to use until 1957. That was when, at last, the chance came to grow plants for love, rather than for profit. It had begun with some experimental beds for hardy perennials, fashioned informally in a large, derelict lawn, in the belief that the conventional herbaceous border was inherently faulty. The long, narrow border with a backing was conducive to spindly growth of plants, due to lack of air, and maybe light as well, for subjects for which an open situation was more natural. The conventional border nearly always became overcrowded, making access for such chores as staking difficult. It was a vicious circle. Plants competing for limited light and air became spindly, and thus needed more staking, with the taller kinds at the rear, overhanging or drawing up the shorter ones in front. My new beds were therefore dug out as islands in the sward, and I stocked them with groups of the tallest-growing kinds in the middle parts, grading down heights to the outsides.

It worked. Only a small fraction of kinds needed staking, for everything grew more sturdily, but less tall than in the conventional borders I'd previously had. Rational spacing and height grading allowed not only more light and air to promote strong, reliable growth, and made for better access for the much reduced maintenance work, but the all-round view of a bed was far more pleasing. With the success of this method of growing perennials beyond doubt, there came an urge to expand into the nearby meadow, with its undulations and fine old trees. All I had to do was to carve out more beds, shaping them to marry in with the existing natural features. It was to be a private garden, where after over thirty years of being almost entirely geared to commercial horticulture, I could at last indulge in growing plants for their own sakes. The loamy soil, enriched with the humus of centuries-old turf, was clay-based, but overlying sand made it easy to work, and it was neutral enough to grow most lime-hating plants which till now had been out of reach of collecting urges. I had no long-term master-plan to go by, for it could only be a more or less spare time hobby task, with myself as the planner and chief digger and planter. It was done bed by bed, as time allowed, and as the collection of plants increased. There were six or seven acres of the meadow to go at, including the Dell, which with the score or more of large oaks, elms, sycamores, and limes ruled out its value as nursery land.

It was while collecting plants to set in the new beds that the term "Desiderata" began to be used. No large garden existed in Britain where Hardy Perennials were

These island beds were planted after the area had been undulated.

given pride of place, and my ambition to make such a garden grew as I discovered now many out-of-the-ordinary species existed in out-of-the-way places. Some were in private gardens in the care of an enthusiastic owner who, if space was lacking, as it often was, had swopped with other owners with the collecting urge. I was by no means the only one keen enough on hardy plants to widen a collection, but was blessed with almost unlimited scope, so that swops with such collectors were easy to make, and much was to be learned from their experiences with subjects new to me. In the process of seeking out these enthusiasts and inviting them back, Flora and I made many friends, and this was how we met such kindred spirits as Margery Fish—who sent us on to others in the South West, like Norman Hadden and Bertram Anderson, till we had a circle of friends and correspondents from Perth to Penzance.

Though nurseries carrying a wider variety of perennials than we already grew scarcely existed, there were several Botanic Gardens where we were made welcome. Swops with these were on a much larger scale, for amongst the beds of various plant families not grown for display I was able to note down a good many unusual species which I thought had claims to garden worthiness. It was the swopping lists, mainly with Botanic Gardens—Edinburgh, Kew, Cambridge and Dublin— that went under the heading of "Desiderata". With Latin as the international language for botanists, it was also used by overseas gardens we visited. Munich, Hanover and Gothenburg were richly stocked with rare kinds we had not seen anywhere else.

Seed lists came in response to my requests from a dozen or so other Botanic Gardens, including some in Russia, and most of these included blank forms headed "Desiderata"—to be filled in for packets of seed of any items we wished to have.

Thus the garden grew, bed by bed, between 1957 and 1962, by which time there were forty-six Island Beds, occupying five acres, and containing about five thousand species and varieties of plants, Some were mere filmy mats of surface growth, like the redolent Mentha *requinii*, with mauve flowers scarcely larger than a pin head, to such giants, seven or eight feet high, as Eupatorium *purpureum* and Inula *magnifica*. And nearly all had been acquired without the medium of money.

'The Dell'.   *Michael Warren*

Deinanthe, Dierama, Disporum, Dodecantheon, Dactylorrhiza (Orchis) and Diplarrhena were amongst the newcomers, which flourished just as well as the much commoner Digitalis and Doronicum. Dicentra grew to a perfection I'd never seen before as a nurseryman, and a self-sown seedling appeared from the American variety of D. *eximia* 'Bountiful', which was deeper in colour and freer in flower. To this was given the name of my younger son, Adrian, about the time he came home for good after his wanderings abroad.

The true "Bleeding Heart", Dicentra *spectabilis,* is surely one of the most entrancing of hardy perennials. Given reasonably good, deep soil, and placed where the fiercest spring winds will not tear at its delicate foliage, it will give joy for years. Its other non-botanic name is "Lady in the Bath", but to see her thus one has to pick off a dangling pink and red locket and hold it upside down, when the flesh pink part becomes the lady, sitting sedately in a deep red bath.

Dierama is the "Fairy's Wand", so named because its slender, three-foot stems, rising from a dense cluster of grassy foliage, arch over so that its tip dangles with pink trumpet-shaped flowers. This, and Deinanthe *coerulea* dislike lime and dry soil, and Deinanthe prefers some shade as well. Its rounded, felty leaves make a low mound, and above, at six to eight inches, come violet blue blobs which also dangle, and though quite charming, the droop obscures the beauty within its waxy petals.

Very few Disporums are seen in gardens. They are woodlanders of the Lily family, but with no superficial resemblance, and are best grown in light shade where not too dry. Of the three or four species I've grown, D. *oreganum* has proved quite reliable. It forms a clumpy, tangle-rooted plant, and sends up fresh, green, pointed leaves and stems to nine inches or so, carrying rather insignificant greenish-white flowers in spring which develop into fruit on fading. By September it is quite attractive as a low bush carrying a show of orange-coloured, cherry-size berries.

Dodecantheons are also woodland plants from North America, where they go by the apt name of "Shooting Star". Red or rosy-purple flowers, which have petals reflexed to such an extent that they show bright orange stamens like the tail of a rocket, come on 9 to 15 inch stems in May and June. These cousins of the Primula are not at all difficult to grow in partial shade, and though out of sight, with dormant fangy roots below ground from August to March, they are not very demanding for what they give by way of display. Many of the thirty or so species in existence will make this display, though only a very few can be seen catalogued for sale.

Doronicums are spurned by some as being common. They are common simply because they are so easy and adaptable, but should not be despised on that account, since they make such a cheerful splash of yellow in spring. The first, D. *caucasicum,* and its variants, are often showing colour in March, and the twelve inch 'Spring

Beauty' is extra good, being fully double. I went a bundle on this during the late 1950s, having been offered by its Danish raiser the distribution rights for the U.K., and it sells even faster now than when it was such a novelty.

Digitalis too are common. As Foxgloves few of them are in any sense perennials. They are amongst the easiest plants to raise from seed, and some will naturalize if left alone. In 1969 I dotted about fifty plants amongst wild Rhododendrons growing beneath tall oaks and pines in a three-acre wood through which I'd laid a narrow gauge, steam-hauled railway for visitors. There this 'Excelsior' strain have seeded themselves ever since in the dry, sandy soil, persisting far better than several other subjects, including ferns, for which I hand-dug several more open spots, most of the contents of which were ruined by rabbits and encroaching nettles. Two perennial Digitalis are worth growing. One is the hybrid *mertonensis* which grows leafily to three feet or so, and has flowers the colour of crushed strawberries. D. *embigua* is shorter and more slender in habit, but the primrose-yellow pouches carry on for several weeks.

Drabas and Douglasias are truly alpine in character. Outdoors a bed or rock garden with a gritty scree mixture is needed to grow such Drabas as *imbricata*, *mollisima*, *rigida* and several more. They form tight hummocks, sometimes grey-green, and in early spring make a charming display in miniature of yellow flowers — some only an inch or two above ground. They need to be in full sun, and with perfect drainage will slowly expand and remain compact for years — or they can be grown in pans in an alpine house. Douglasias are also considered choice Alpines for the connoisseur, and but for the yellow-flowered D. *vitaliana* are seldom seen, much less offered. The habit of D. *vitaliana* is rather similar to that of a Draba, though it is quite unrelated. The flowers nestle on the close mat formation at virtually no height at all. The generic name is in honour of David Douglas, (1798-1834), who as a young man was sent to Western North America as a collector by the Royal Horticultural Society. He was a strange and often lonely man, with his ambition sometimes embarrassingly in conflict with his inbred self-effacement and introversion. But he was dedicated, and very productive as a collector, despite the loss of all he'd collected and noted on one expedition up the Colombia river, when he barely escaped with his life after some rapids sank his boat. Such dangers he could face fearlessly, but he was afraid of cattle, especially bulls. What he must have felt when, walking alone on one of the Hawaiian Islands, he fell into a pit trap to find a wild bull already inside is beyond imagination, for this time there was no escape for him.

I too am afraid of bulls, having been chased by one as a boy. I steer clear, too, of angry swine, but once in Ontario had the job of driving out a 25 stone hog, due to be knifed, which had stumbled into a trench I was digging, four feet deep, in which to lay water pipes. I was thankful when its owner came to help.

Delphiniums are a rather sad and sorry story for me. Although I would dispute the claim made by some that they are "Queen of Border Plants", there was a time when there was some prestige amongst nurserymen who grew named varieties. There was then a good demand for them, and since they could only be produced from cuttings, they were worth twice as much as the more ordinary run of plants. Blackmore and Langdon of Bath were the top specialists as raisers of new varieties, and their exhibits were a byword in magnificence at flower shows. Bakers of Codsall and Bees of Chester, Artindales of Boston, and a few lesser firms also put up splendid displays in the 1920s and '30s. It did not seem to matter in those days if garden subjects were labour-demanding. Delphiniums certainly were that, needing rich soil and much staking to make them give of their best.

Having gone in for wholesale-only production in 1934 my ambitions naturally took in named Delphiniums, despite the cost of plants from which to work up stocks. At that time it was cheaper to buy stock plants from Holland, and the hundred pounds' worth I imported was the largest outlay I'd ever made on a purchase of plants. They were standard rather than the most up-to-date novelties, and as I'd had no previous experience with them I bedded them in under glass, on a horticultural friend's recommendation, so as to take an early batch of cuttings, to be followed by another when more growth came. The cuttings, knifed off with a firm base, were put in cold frames, but by the time these were showing signs of rooting the stock plants were fast rotting away, through Black Rot. My friend had forgotten to warn me to use a preventative, and I'd not known of their susceptibility. Black Rot then infected the framed cuttings, some of which had rooted, but it was checked by Cheshunt Compound. The survivors were planted out, and though these were very few more in number than the stock plants from which they were taken, they grew well enough to make me decide to try again.

That year, 1935, I joined the newly-formed British Delphinium Society, went to meetings, shows and outings, and studied literature on them. Another purchase of stock plants, along with what I had already, were cut up into rooted divisions. Cuttings, I decided, were too risky. These also grew well, until I was caught out again by my own over-enthusiasm as a propagator. Sir Roland Biffen of Cambridge was an agricultural scientist with a love of plants, and an experimentor with them. He told me he'd succeeded in propagating Delphiniums by cutting out, after flowering, immature eyes which would have become flowering spikes the following year. As a method he reckoned it would yield more rapid increase than any other. A wet spell in July, 1936 was propitious, and in digging up a few plants for the sake of these eyes, I found them capable of being divided as well. So it was that several thousand more were dug and divided, and replanting more than doubled the total. But by autumn the replants had made so little growth that they were unfit for sale, and scarcely any of the eyes had grown at all.

I could but blame myself for being both ignorant and greedy, but enough undisturbed plants were left to try from cuttings again the following spring. These were placed straight into frames from the field, and Black Rot was kept at bay with Cheshunt Compound waterings—as well as dipping the cuttings in it before insertion. The results were good, but there was a long way to go yet. My aim was to have a stock of at least fifty thousand in fifty named varieties to catalogue, and this meant yet more to buy for stock. By 1939 the target was reached, but there was scarcely any demand when autumn came. Not even a 25 per cent reduction on the 1,872 different kinds of Perennials and Alpines, including Delphiniums, tempted our customers to buy. Not could I blame them for it seemed certain that total war would lead to total food production as far as nurserymen were concerned. In the spring of 1940 began the task of destroying plants to make way for carrots, onions, tomatoes and such like, but though I left the Delphiniums almost till last, they were too large for sale anyway, even had there been any orders for them in autumn 1941 and spring 1942.

A nucleus of about three thousand were left, and with hopes of sales picking up as victory came in sight, a few were replanted for sale. By then I'd decided not to return to Oakington to live, but when in 1946 I purchased Bressingham Hall Farm it needed will power to rebuild stocks of plants, cut down as they were to less than the required 15 per cent of pre-war acreage. The fifty-mile move was slow, tedious and worrying during that grim winter. Frost prevented lifting many open ground plants till late March, and when the Delphinium remnants and another Dutch consignment arrived, they were priority. Both cuttings and divisions boosted quantities to about 25,000. Because of recent floods they had to be planted on newly-ploughed grassland, and with drought following looked pretty sick. Watering did not prevent the steady loss which by June was evident, and when the irrigation nozzles became blocked with algae from the river, it was also evident that they were under attack from unsuspected wireworm. An S.O.S. to the suppliers of wireworm killer met with a quick response, but still the Delphiniums died. I made tests, which ended in the suppliers admitting they'd sent the wrong stuff. But by the time the correct compound finally arrived and had worked into the soil more than half the plants were dead.

This would have been the time to give up growing named Delphiniums as a bad job. But I stubbornly went on, believing there was a demand to be met. Some were sold whilst I was in Canada, with too little regard to retaining plants for stock. On my return, there was no money to buy more, but slowly, using proven methods, both quantities and varieties increased, though the Bressingham soil did not suit them so well as Oakington. Each year we had to pick out the largest for sale, leaving the smaller, less productive and vigorous plants for stock. But in my rather obstinate persistence I scarcely took notice of changes that were slowly taking place. Sales had declined I thought, because we could not seem to produce enough quality plants to meet the demand, despite the use of F.Y.M. and fertilizer. But by this time American breeders had produced Delphiniums which came reasonably true to colour from seed. We were being asked for them, and in growing more for sale — at a much lower cost than named varieites from cuttings or division — it dawned on me that times were changing, and that because of their high labour requirements as garden plants garden owners wanted shorter-growing Delphiniums. And they saw better value in the much cheaper ones from seed. So too did I, as I experimented with my Island Beds in the garden. I realised too that it was Delphiniums more than any other subject which, because of the catastrophic effects of any neglect of staking in the conventional borders I'd previously tended, had made me think of Island Beds. Not that Delphiniums in the latter obviated the need to support their heavy spikes. They were by far the most troublesome in this respect wherever they were planted, and any attempt to skimp that tedious chore was invariably caught out by the first strong winds of summer. Once felled by wind a Delphinium spike can very seldom be restored to its regal state, and will often snap in the attempt.

I still have a few named varieties in garden groups — and if I remember to stake them in May they are a splendid sight in June and July. They are longer lived as plants than the Pacific Hybrids which come from seed, for some of mine have remained undisturbed for a dozen years. I'll let them stay, if only as a memorial to lost labours. But if by 1974 I could no longer hold from giving permission for those remaining on the nursery to be scrapped, there was and still is something of a pang when memories go back over the past forty years of struggling with them. It is eased only when I reflect that they would show up on the debit side of a profit and loss account for the nursery, and that apart from the persistently champion specialists of Blackhouse and Langdon, practically every other nursery in England has also given up growing named varieties other than from seed.

CHAPTER FIVE

Erigeron, Excavagating . . . .

EXCAVATING, digging and delving, one way and another, for something or other, has occupied a fairly large slice of my life. As a boy I enjoyed digging holes, fascinated by gravel or water, or whatever else might turn up from below. Later, digging in preparation for planting appealed as a worth-while job, but in digging virgin soil there was added zest, especially if something from antiquity might be revealed. Two winters at Oakington were spent in trenching over, two spits deep, an unlevel meadow my parents had acquired. It was slow work—and I cannot imagine how it was that neither my father nor I thought to count the cost. Even with basic wages then at thirty shillings a week, it could have been seen as costing far more to dig by hand than the price of the land, which was £65 per acre. Of course digging was more effective in levelling off the dips and hummocks than ploughing, but with only about three acres dug after those two winters' work, the rest had to be ploughed. In a hollow we found skeletons, with a shield and weapons, which the antiquarians said proved it to be the scene of a skirmish between the natives and the invading Danes, who sacked the district in 870 A.D.

Not far away, I enlisted my helpers in digging by hand a small pond, a few years later. The field proved to be poorly drained in places, and my idea was to make the pond in a low place to act as a sump, by leading into it pipe drains from wherever the winter water table was too high. Although this meant more digging for me, I enjoyed the job, and it allowed me to grow moisture-loving plants beside the pond. At Oakington I also dug two wells and many pits, in order to use the sand and gravel for paths, pottings and plunge beds, until I realized it was cheaper to have it delivered in, but the wells were essential as an irrigation water supply.

My farm in Burwell Fen was below river level, and much of it became flooded within weeks of me becoming owner. In places the underlying peat was eight feet deep. It would have been a pleasure to dig dykes if the water could be induced to run away, but it was not until 1941 that it did so effectively, as a result of the district pumping system being overhauled. By then I'd taken on three hundred acres of derelict land adjoining, to reclaim it for food production, so that with miles of new dykes to be dug I was much in contact with digging and diggers.

Having moved to Fordham late in 1941 to be nearer the farm, now expanded to 540 acres, I had the pleasure of digging a new half-acre garden. My father, now turned seventy, retired, and with my mother cared for my three small children whilst I was away at the farm all day. In the light evenings Father and I dug and planted little by little; he for Primroses and other favourites, and I for mine which I'd rescued from Oakington, where the thirty-six acre nursery had been turned over to nearly ninety per cent food production, with visits from me needed only once or twice a week.

So much of my life as a digger has been either to be rid of water in order to cultivate, or to bring it in where it was needed for irrigation. Both used up a large amount of my energy after coming to Bressingham. After the flood of March, 1947, trenches had to be dug and pipe drains laid in April, in order to make land fit for planting. No sooner had this phase ended than a drought set in, making it necessary to dig more trenches and lay more pipes — of a different kind — to use river water for irrigating land we'd just drained. This was largely a failure, because weed and algae from the river blocked the spray line nozzles, and it was not until July, when a borehole permit was finally granted, that clean water was available. By then it was too late for many thousands of plants.

Having dug most of the two-acre pond, by way of a change in 1955, and acquired a mechanical digger for the ditches, there was only occasional spade work for me after that, though I mostly carried a spade when I walked the fields, just in case. The pleasure of letting water go — even if only puddles — and of applying it to plants in need has never left me. To see plants suffering from thirst affects me with a peculiar hurt on their behalf, and I have to do something about it if I possibly can. For the new Island Beds at Bressingham water pipes spread out underground to meet irrigation needs. With fear of both drought and flood removed, digging these new beds was a pleasure. The average rainfall here is under twenty-four inches, and the drought of 1959 was so severe that in September, when I marked out a new bed to be dug, I had to let a hose-pipe run for hours before a spade could penetrate. The method when digging what had been grassland for generations was to mark out the shape with sticks, and then chop up the turf with a rotavator to three or four inches deep. An opening trench was then dug, and with a full spit of clean soil covering the chopped-up turf in the trench, the latter caused no trouble with cavities as it rotted and shrank, as would have been the case if burying large pieces of turf — a lesson learned to our cost when trenching the meadow at Oakington years before, when cavities were sometimes left well below, which hindered root growth.

There's a little tale to tell about Erigerons. I'd always had liking for the rich, orange shades to be seen in E. *aurantiacus,* which sends its rayed daisy flowers up on stems ten to twenty inches tall from May to July. Its fault is that of being short-lived, though not merely an annual, and with lavender to pink shades predominating in other kinds, which were reliably perennial, I asked Percy to fiddle with them, in the hope of obtaining more colourful breaks. He did so whilst I was in Canada, and by 1951 had raised some seedlings from his crosses. He had not recorded on paper what he'd used as parents, but there were marked differences in growth, and when they flowered again in 1952 there were scarcely two alike in colour. A few were orange flowered, but these still had the habit of E. *aurantiacus,* which steadily lost vigour after the first flowering. Not so some of the pink-flowered ones, which were quite exciting. These, and some lavender, violet and mauve seedlings, were vigorous and free-flowering, and the usual process of staking the best began.

By 1953 it was time to think about launching them, and a selection was sent for trial at Wisley under number, so that names could be given to those that came out best. But for some reason the Judging Committee deferred a decision till 1955, instead of 1954 as I'd hoped. The quandary was to know whether to wait another year, or to name what I considered to be the best, because intensive propagating had given us ample stocks to launch them in the 1954 catalogue. I couldn't wait, and although I'd intended to name only four or five of the most distinctive, I had to choose eight, in case the Committee gave awards to some I'd ruled out. To mark their origin as a new breed, each name ended in "ity"; from 'Dimity' the dwarfest, to 'Festivity' the tallest at just over two feet. They sold quite well in that first year, but in the following year, when some Awards of Merit and Highly Commended were given at the R.H.S. trial, I realized too late that there were now too many "itys". It was a pity, but over the years they have become sorted out and reduced by the natural process of survival of the fittest. Some must have had more of the inherent weakness of E. *aurantiacus* than I'd imagined, and although I persisted for several years with seedlings of the latter, staking the brightest and best orange shades, and dividing the survivors, always in hope that some would prove persistently perennial, none ever survived more than two or three flowerings. Nor can I imagine now that such a factor can ever be achieved. It may not be safe to generalize, but there are so many examples of perennial vigour in plants being reduced by breeding or hybridizing for the sake of improved flowering that it must be contrary to some law to expect the reverse to occur.

One of the few biennials I grow is Eryngium *giganteum.* At least one knows that this will die after one flowering, to be termed monocarpic, rather than annual or biennial. As with nearly all short-lived plants it comes easily from seed, and sometimes self-sown plants will appear, like a silver-leaved, thistly rosette. The flowering stem is silvery-blue, almost the colour of wood-ash, with a slightly bluer tint in the teasle-like flowering bracts, which come on stiffly-branching stems three feet or more tall. Seen in the dusk it is rather eerie — enough so for someone to coin for it the modern common name of "Miss Willmott's Ghost".

The flowers of Eryngiums, and Erigerons, along with other plants in blue and lavender, have a special quality when seen as daylight fades on summer evenings. The deeper colours — reds, purple and orange — as well as foliage greenery, become dark and less distinguishable, but not so the blues, which become ethereal and opaque, as if the darkening sky brings out a depth undiscerned in broad daylight.

Then the subtle differences between pure blue, through the lighter lavender, mauve or amethyst shadings are plain enough to discern, but in the gloaming they become bewitched. So do our cats when in the garden with us; scampering around, then hiding beneath and between the plants, to spring out at us as we pass by. I have never bothered to seek an explanation for this phenomenon of changing colours. It gives the garden an air of mystery — a secret, fleetingly revealed, to be absorbed by one's more emotional or aesthetic senses, best not explained in technical terms lest it loses thereby something of its value and quality.

There is a variant of Campanula *macratha* to which I gave the name 'Gloaming' a few years ago. In daylight its flowers, topping sturdy, four-foot stems, need to be seen at fairly close quarters to appreciate the colour, for it is the palest violet-blue imaginable, altogether charming. But in the late evening it becomes quite outstanding against the darkening green background, and my choice of a name seemed apt. Not far from my group of 'Gloaming' stands, as a background, three Cornus *kousa* 'chinensis', growing as a group. After fourteen years' growth they are ten or twelve feet high, and from June to August carry waxy, creamy-white flowers about two inches across. These show up at any time of day, and are luminous enough to be seen all through the midsummer night as well. This and Rubus 'Tridel', also white, are subjects I would not be without, even though shrubs have never been my speciality as a cultivator and collector.

Aruncus *sylvester* — Goats Beard.

White-flowered subjects are essential in a garden to achieve an overall balance of colour, especially if green backgrounds exist. Amongst other perennials that achieve this contrast is Aruncus *sylvester,* which flowers in early summer, with cloudy spikes of milky-white reaching over six feet where soil is rich or damp. Its fault is that of having too brief a flowering-period, but with abundant subsequent greenery it has the edge on Crambe *cordifolia.* This branches widely to carry numberless pure white flowers above cabbagy leaves, also in early summer. While it lasts it is outstanding, but with fading leaves a drab gap for the rest of the year. Towards the end of summer Artemisia *lactiflora* comes into focus as a telling background subject. It has erect, crowded stems to four feet or so, well clothed in jagged green leaves, and from August to October the whole plant is crowned with creamy-white plumes made up of tiny florets.

These, to my mind, are far more garden-worthy than the more commonly seen Shasta Daisies—Chrysanthemum *maximum.* I have something of an aversion to them, which I know amounts to prejudice because as a boy and youth I handled so many as cut flowers for market. I could never enthuse, either as nurseryman or gardener, over the doubles when they evolved. The first, raised in Norfolk in the early 1930s, was 'Esther Read', and it has been quite a money-spinner for many a grower since then. It became so ubiquitous as a florists' flower that even non-professionals dropped its generic name as if it had no other than just 'Esther Read'. But I've also heard of people who believed that the colours in which it is often sold or used for wreathmaking were natural variations, not aware that the blue, pink and yellow 'Esther Reads' were dyed. There was—and perhaps still is—one double variety named 'Cobham Gold' raised, I believe, by the late Lord Darnley, but the only natural yellow is to be seen, very faintly in its centre, if you look for it. So the reason why scarcely any Chrysanthemum *maximum* are to be seen in my garden is mainly because I became fed up, forty to fifty years ago, with cutting them, stripping off the stinking lower leaves, to bunch, water, and push them in boxes, to be tied with sisal string which brought blisters to one's hands. The only one in which I saw beauty was a slender-stemmed, more gracefully-rayed single flower; and early variety named 'Rentpayer'. As a cut flower it was quite widely grown in the early 1920s, but having searched for it in vain in recent years, I fear it must now be lost to cultivation.

Many gardeners no doubt have their likes and dislikes, and the latter are probably due to some prejudice incurred by past experiences with certain plants and flowers. Or perhaps just to be different. This is largely so in my case, having had and stuck to the urge to grow hardy plants which have suffered from undeserved neglect. To be single-minded in this way, knowing that the scope is wider than can be filled in a lifetime, I have no time or inclination to go in for such things as Dahlias, Gladiolus, or even Rhododendrons and Roses, which can be seen in abundance elsewhere.

The Author's first flint building project: building a bridge for the Dell Garden, 1957.

CHAPTER SIX

Flint, Fuchsia . . . .

M Y WORKING life has not been so entirely dedicated as have most professional gardeners. My venture into farming and land reclamation between 1939 and 1945 was so demanding that plants became more of a recreation. Then came the Canadian interlude, followed by several years' hard graft as a nurseryman, but having at last become involved deeply in garden making and collecting out-of-the-way plants, I found the need for recreation again, by way of a change from almost total committment. I see it as a kind of flaw in my make-up to plunge in up to the neck in most things I tackle.

Building with flint in the garden came unexpectedly as a means of recreation during the garden-making period of 1958-1962. A bricklayer engaged to construct a bridge over a sunken path ran out of suitable bricks. I asked him to finish off with flints—of which so many East Anglian churches and houses were constructed. But the bricklayer tried to lay flints as he would lay bricks. The effect wasn't at all pleasing, and I had to ask him to stop. A few days later, when alone, I tried to find a better way, and gradually, through trial and error it came. My method was to make these very unevenly-shaped stones fit together so as to expose the minimum of cement. They had varying colours as well as shapes—white, buff, bluish-grey, sandy-orange, and black. By cracking some large, awkward stones the shiny black interior could then be used to face outwards, to give variety in both size and colour. But if it took time, because of having to sort through the pile of stones before finding one that would fit the next space to be filled, it was very rewarding. It was also mentally relaxing, in the same way as is a jigsaw puzzle, with the difference that the wall would be a permanent garden feature. During the next three years at odd times, I built about two hundred yards of retaining walls up to about 4½-feet high, to fit in with the undulating landscape. I also built a round hut as a shelter-cum-summer house. Its walls, eight feet high, had to be faced both within and without, and by the time its conical roof was thatched over an arched doorway, many a summer evening had slipped by, when probably I could have been hoeing.

The last of the walls was begun in autumn, 1962. Never being able to spend more than a few hours daily on it, the task dragged on into winter. New work had to be covered with straw and sacks to prevent frost damage, but by New Year it was completed, and very soon after frost settled down in earnest.

People who say summers are not so hot, nor winters so frosty as they used to be, do so because it is these that stand out in their memories. They tend to forget the

The summer house and retaining wall built in 1960 by the author.

ordinary summers and relatively mild winters in between. By 1963 I could remember quite vividly the half dozen or so sharp winters occurring in the previous fifty years, but apart from that of 1947, none had gripped so hard as 1963. With no snow cover at Bressingham the soil froze deeply — two feet down in places. The soil surface became parched-looking, as if it was a drought — as indeed it was for six weeks. Plant growth above ground was seared, and even Hollies and Ivies drooped their leaves in agony. The toll was heavy. Some plants — including Iris *stylosa*, Kniphofias, Pampas Grass and others never recovered. Others showed no sign of life till midsummer, and severe losses occurred also where autumn nursery plantings had been lifted out of the ground by frost action, and lay with their roots exposed too long before replanting was possible. One pair of large, north-facing beds were covered in an inch-thick layer of ice, where a film of snow had drifted onto the solidly-frozen ground, to turn into slush in a temporary thaw, before freezing up once more. None, it seemed, of the hundred and fifty different kinds of plants they contained could possibly survive, and yet when spring finally came, all but Salvia *uliginosa* came through. Resolving never to be caught again, everything that suffered in 1963 was thereafter given winter protection. Straw from the farm had to be spread out by the end of November on two or three acres of the nursery, as well as around certain groups in the garden. By mid-March it had to be carted off again, and this routine had been followed in the twelve winters since then, during none of which has there been a frost that would have caused any harm.

Floods have never afflicted the garden, but disaster struck the nursery in September, 1968. There had been drainage difficulties on several occasions in nursery fields in the peaty valley bottom. With water under control plants grew splendidly, but it was a chancy business, due to the valley being within a bottle-necked river outfall. One year 30,000 recently-planted young Helleborus *niger* were ruined by a minor flood. On another occasion when a small flood came in advance of a frosty spell, our collection of Phlox, covering two or three acres, had to be dug up in a hurry from beneath a canopy of "cat's ice", left suspended as the water below soaked down or ran off.

By September, 1968, with about fifteen acres of valley land under nursery, such subjects as Astilbe, Trollius, Phlox and many more were still in full growth. They had never looked so good, and a pile of orders was waiting for them a few days before lifting was due to begin. Rain began one Sunday at midday. By next morning 4.38 inches was recorded at the official register in the garden, and by that evening the valley was covered by water up to two feet deep. The bottle-necked river could not cope. Floods lower down in the Waveney Valley held ours back, and it took ten days to clear, by which time most of those plants, being in full leaf, were drowned.

Frost and flood. By way of contrast, fire too can be a menace on that peaty land. A neighbour once cleared a six-acre wood of Alder, Poplar and Willow. All useful timber was sold, but stumps and waste were bulldozed into a corner and a

The garden in winter.

fire was lit which, it was hoped, would burn them up. It did, but it took four years, for the fire found the underlying peat, and slowly penetrated beneath the stumps, drying them out as they sank down into the creeping fire, to be slowly consumed. On damp days a little steam could be seen rising down there, and with the wind in the right direction came whiffs of acrid smell, just to show that year in, year out, the fire was still burning. When we purchased the field, and if half an acre of it was ruined as grazing land, we made good use of the ash the fire left behind. It was the flood of 1968 which finally extinguished it.

An old timer once told me that too much water was more lethal to plant life than too little. Though I knew he was referring mainly to potted plants, I was inclined to disbelieve him, and it has taken years of experience, often costly, to realize that this applies to most outdoor subjects as well. Yet there are districts having a far heavier annual rainfall than dry East Anglia, where plants do not die from excessive wet. So much depends on drainage and soil porosity, and many of the winter losses in my garden are due to lack of it. The soil is good, but it compacts when wet because of the fine sand in the soil, which also contains clay. Even on the black, peaty soil of the valley bottom this same problem occurs, reducing porosity from the effect of heavy rain and irrigation, and from men's feet and machine's wheels. Hardiness is, I am now sure, affected by drainage. Porous, free-draining soils are less likely to freeze solid than wet, congealed soil.

The Francoas are on the borderline of hardiness, and F. *racemosa*, known as "Bridal Wreath", was an old-time favourite as a window plant. I grew it outdoors, along with F. *sonchifolia* and F. *appendiculata*, for several years, but found them far less hardy in tight soil than in the lee of conifers whose roots kept the soil more open. Francoas are attractive both for foliage and flowering. The latter come in spray-like spikes up to two feet, of near-white or light pink flowers, somewhat akin, but much more graceful than Bergenia, in June and July. Leaves are soft, long, crinkled and indented. They do best in some shade, and flourish in leafy or peaty soil.

Filipendulas—the herbaceous Spireas—took their new generic name from a species Spirea *filipendula*. It is now F. *hexapetala*, and is one of the few that will flourish in quite dry soil, whereas the rest like it damp. The double F. *hexapetala* 'plena' is dazzlingly white, on cloudy heads about two feet high in June to July, above very pretty deep green carroty foliage. It is a very good garden plant, as is the slightly taller, larger F. *h.* 'grandiflora', flowering at about the same time, creamy white and scented of Meadowsweet. The latter is F. *ulmaria*, and if it were not so abundant in the wild, I quite think it would be cultivated in gardens. There is a form with patchy variegations in the leaves, but I do not rate this as at all outstanding.

A really good all-golden leaved subject, however, goes under the name of F. *ulmaria* 'Aurea', though I have my doubts as to whether this is correctly classified. Given some shade, in good, not dry soil, it will make a mound of brightly-golden foliage from April to November, but its flowers are insignificant, and are best cut down to encourage leafiness. It shares with non-natives a liking for moist but not boggy, saturated soil, and amongst these is the six-foot Filipendula *venusta* 'magnifica' (syn rubra). This will grow with gusto in sun or shade, but in some shade the wide heads of glistening pink flowers will last longer. This same proviso applies to the charming, fingery-leaved F. *digitata* 'nana', which seldom exceeds 18 inches, with dense heads of deep rose pink, and the choice F. *purpurea*, (syn F. *palmata* 'rubra', which is twice that height and has flowers of cherry red. F. *elegantissima* reaches about three feet, strong and bushy, also rose-pink, but the six to nine foot F. *gigantea* is difficult to place and flowering is brief. As with most subjects with a preference for rich, moist soil, these Filipendulas vary in height according to the treatment they are given.

Fuchsias are far hardier than most people imagine. I grew up with the handed-down belief that the only hardy Fuchsia was what was then known as F. *riccartoni*— now F. *magellanica*. As a native of Tierra del Fuego it should be, but hybrids have very mixed blood. At any rate, such varieties as 'Dr Foerster', 'Eva Borg' and 'Mrs Popple', to name only a few, are reliably hardy, especially if planted deeply at the outset. This is largely the secret of survival, and the new shoots spring up from below in May, by which time it is safe to cut last year's above-ground growth hard back. By August they will be in full growth, and will mostly flower continuously until frosts come again. These are such distinctive plants, with their dangling flowers in rich reds and pinks, often bi-coloured, and more worth growing because they come after the garden is losing its high summer glory.

It jars on the sensibilities of both Flora and me to hear early visitors to the garden come out with, "It will look nice in a few weeks, when it's all in flower". Perhaps they are at a loss to know what else to say, but such remarks are rather fatuous. In any garden where a reasonably wide variety is grown the greatest joy for the beholder should be in the appreciation of not only what may be in flower, but of what else holds promise. Some of us become excited at the first signs of renewed growth in early spring. And as the days lengthen one by one the harbingers reveal their beauty, even if it lies in grace or form rather than colour. A blaze of colour is for many of us not the only criterion, and the sight of fields of Tulips is not half so moving as a garden in which less colour and more variety is to be seen. The casual viewer might not notice the subtle appeal of plants in a great variety of form and in many stages of development. The real lover of plants wanders slowly past them pausing, with observant, appreciative gaze, peering, wondering and marvelling at what is to be seen.

It is mostly about Tulip time when our garden is first open each year to the public. It is then that those whose eye is for not much else than sheer colour is apt to come out with the prediction of how much brighter it will appear in July and

August — as if a quick glance is enough in April or May. But no matter how richly the promise of spring is rewarded, with the arrival of full summer glory, this deeper sense of anticipation and appreciation is apt to become diminished, as is an appetite with a feast. Not that such a metaphor is really applicable, because a true gardener never loses the element of hope and anticipation. As one season follows another there is always something to look forward to, even if it's work to be done when autumn fading comes, that should enhance the prospect and bounties of an unborn year.

This applies not only to decorative gardening. For fruit and vegetables too one must plan and work well in advance. It is all part of our role of having to work in with nature, of having to abide by the rules by which all cultivators, including the farmers, are circumscribed. As Fragaria, Strawberries can be an example. To ensure a crop of luscious fruit in summer, the soil needs preparation nearly a year in advance. Runners on old plants have to be cut off not many weeks after the last berry has been picked, and a new bed should be planted in September. In spring it needs hoeing and fertilizing, and the abundance of flowers in May holds the promise of fruit in June and July, allowing for such hazards as late frosts causing damage. The whole process is one of hopeful anticipation, provided the rules have been kept. But the Blackbird, whose song we love to hear, is also fond of Strawberries, and cannot be blamed for having a picking at our expense, because he too is but taking advantage of nature's bounty. We place nets over our Strawberry bed, but having a touch of sentiment where songbirds are concerned, I mostly arrange to have an extra row of strawberries planted, outside those netted for ourselves, just for the birds.

Maybe I'm soft, and not only in this way. One reason why I prefer digging with a fork and not a spade is that there is less risk of chopping through a worm. A worm may not have any feelings, but I have, if I see one cut in half and writhing, as if in agony. Yet when I'm digging in winter, when birds are hungry, I can happily flip a worm over to a nearby Robin or Blackbird to be swallowed whole. Field mice can do quite a lot of damage, eating certain bulbs and seeds, but I can no longer chase one I've disturbed and bash it to death as I once would have.

CHAPTER SEVEN

Gentian, Geranium . . . .

G ARDEN centres and "ground cover" have something in common. Both terms are importations from the U.S.A., and though no doubt they had to come—along with supermarkets—to meet modern needs and trends, their effect is not entirely beneficial to all concerned. The demand for ground cover plants, which producers have met, has made it possible for work-shy garden owners to take an easier way out. But merely to cover the ground with subjects able more or less to look after themselves and smother weeds is not gardening in the true sense. What is gained in time and effort is lost in terms of beauty and interest, because few ground coverers are either beautiful or interesting. Even those that are, become less so to the beholder, who sees them year in, year out till they become boring with sameness.

Variety is as much the spice of gardening as it is of life itself, and where ground coverers are used to the exclusion of the many other, infinitely more interesting subjects in existence, then one of the true joys of gardening is lost. This may be a generalization, but the truth of it will not be lost on either those who know that the extra time and effort a variety demands is amply rewarded, or on those who have become bored by changing over to ground coverers. The latter have their place, but for those who wish to make the most of their gardening space, ground cover plants should be confined to the less favoured spots, where more interesting subjects will not thrive.

Garden centres thrive partly because most garden owners nowadays are more mobile, and partly—perhaps mainly—because they like to see what they are buying. Previous to about 1950 one was obliged to order from either a catalogue or advertisement, or go to a retailing nursery, where little effort was made to assemble saleable lines in one area. It meant quite long tramps inspecting nursery beds, involving time for both seller and buyer. Garden shops existed in towns, but living outdoor plants on sale were necessarily restricted, and so the modern, still proliferating garden centres, often offering a range of nursery products as well as seeds and sundries, naturally attracted buyers. But in meeting a need, they also created a wider horizon in sales, catering as they did for visual appeal. No longer were hardy nursery stock sales confined to autumn and spring, once trees, shrubs and hardy plants became containerized. Not many years ago it would have been impossible to purchase a rose bush in bud or flower to transfer direct to one's garden. But now one can, at a price, and·this tendency is likely to increase, despite the fact that roses and most other shrubs are better planted in the November to March period, dug straight from the field—and at a much lower price than when container grown.

Alan Bloom, with daughter Anthea, in the Dell garden in 1964, by which time it had grown to cover five acres.   *B. Colton*

This example is one of several that could be quoted, but it is not directed against garden centres. It is merely an appeal to gardeners to be discriminating; to realize that there are snags to visual buying. It is so easy to forget that nursery-grown plants, or hard-wood subjects are much less expensive when purchased in the dormant state, without paying for the container and the extra labour involved. It is also a fact that garden centres tend to confine what they offer to subjects having visual sales appeal, dormant or otherwise. But there remain a host of others which do not lend themselves in this way, but are perhaps more attractive when they come into flower. My fear is that these may languish for want of recognition. Nurseries growing them find sales dwindling because buyers go for visual appeal of containerized subjects in garden centres and stores, till they become uneconomic to produce. A nurseryman cannot grow just for love subjects he knows are good; if they do not sell he has to drop them.

A love of plants for their own sakes is shared by what is probably a minority of both amateur and professional gardeners. The number of firms growing a wide variety has diminished greatly in recent years, but one may be sure that those who carry on do so more for love than money. They are nearly all specialists in one way or another and issue a catalogue rather than cater for visual sales. But the dice of economic change seem to be loaded against them—it takes extra labour to grow a wide variety, and other costs are proportionately high if they aim to keep up a high standard of quality.

You can buy gnomes as well as sundials in most garden centres, but you can't buy what Flora calls "Godwotery". By this she means the appealing side-kicks that come to true gardeners. The term comes of course from the oft-used line, "A garden is a lovesome thing, God wot," carved on garden seats and sundials. But it can include anything from the pricks of rose thorns, or the washing of cold, dirty fingers after a weeding job well done, to the joy of planting something one has been wanting for years. It can also be the first white in snowdrops, the blackbird's song, the taste of the season's first strawberry one has grown, seeing a dragonfly on the pool, or the gossamer on a September morn. True gardening embraces sorrows and joys, fatigue and zest, failure and success, hates and loves, through winter and summer, spring and autumn, as with life itself. One becomes immersed, as a part of nature, yet with a second nature to use craft with one's creativeness, to steal a march on nature where it is to our advantage, whilst being aware of one's limitations.

This, and much more besides, is what makes for the deep sense of joy in gardening. It cannot be purchased, and such articles as gnomes, sundials and other man-made objects will not bring it, if one has but a superficial approach or liking for gardening. One has to dig, to plant, to hoe and nurture, to study soil and growth for the practice it gives and the knowledge it brings. Expertise is not essential to achieve this deeper satisfaction, but those who seek it because they have the need or the urge to find it, will do so in time. A sincere beginner is far more likely to find it than the man or woman who spends a small fortune on having a garden made and stocked and tended by others.

Much emphasis has in recent years been placed on trouble-free gardening, by writers of books and articles. I was once persuaded to agree to two of my books having "Trouble-free" as part of the title, though I knew full well there is no such thing as trouble-free gardening in the strict sense. A true gardener does not see caring for plants as trouble, but as an integral part of the pleasure of gardening. Not many readers took me to task over those two books, in which I tried to point out ways and means of reducing unnecessary toil by adopting a more rational approach to the growing of perennials and alpines. No doubt other writers believed people wanted to know ways and means of reducing the amount of labour and trouble in gardening, and this is in keeping with a more general attitude to manual work now prevailing.

But evidence is emerging that manual work is not after all to be shunned and despised. And if it gives some outlet to the creativeness within us, which true gardening certainly does, then it's good for both body and mind. This theme is a long-standing hobby-horse of mine, but I mustn't forget that I'm probably one of the fortunate few, in being able to enjoy my life's work because it holds an element of creativeness. It is, however, true that most forms and expressions of creativeness involve manual work, and that practical gardening is an outstanding example of how mind and body can combine to produce results beneficial to both. It needs only the right mental attitude, so long as one has a body capable of responding to it. Where there's a will, there's a way—and the reward is beyond price to those who find the true pleasures that gardening holds.

Someone I know has found it in growing Gentians as a speciality. The urge to become a gardener did not come to him until quite late in life, but it was the sight of the blue spring Gentian, (G. *verna*), growing in the Alps, that set him off. His first attempts to grow it in his garden were not very successful, but the genus appealed so much that before long he was trying other species as well. He soon learned that those that flowered in spring like lime, but the autumn-flowering did not. The summer-flowering kinds were quite tolerant, and though some were not spectacular, he accumulated about twenty before tackling once more the more fussy early and late-flowering species. The big-trumpeted G. *acaulis* often failed to flower in spring, though the plants grew well, but baffled him year after year as he tried this and that to tempt it to give of its wonderful best. Once or twice over the years it did, but there was no rule of thumb, as he learned of others with a similar experience. He continued trying to keep the much smaller G. *verna* alive, but cussedly this often died out after flowering once. Raising it from seed was a fascinating process, but he gradually lost heart, until a gardening friend recommended cow turds, amply mixed in with a gritty soil on a raised bed in full sun. It worked, and each spring thereafter the sight enchanted him.

By this time he was already dabbling with autumn Gentians, beginning with G. *sino-ornata*. This, and others he tried later, did not like limey soil or full sun, so he dug out a little plot eighteen inches deep in the lee of a wall, and replaced natural limey soil with peat, leafmould and lime-free sand. The slender, thong-like roots, planted in spring—of six different kinds including hybrids—were so small and fragile that it seemed unlikely that they could survive, let alone give a display. But they did, and when September came his reward was there in full glory, a rhapsody in blues.

Gentiana *septemfida* an easy growing, summer flowering, blue species.

More than one gardener I know has become enamoured of hardy Geraniums —
true Geraniums, I mean, not those grown in pots or for summer bedding, which are
correctly Pelagoniums. Only one true Geranium I know is not fully winter hardy,
(G. *traversii*), but the number of species and varieties which are garden-worthy
amount to close on one hundred. In my garden there are over seventy, from the
little rock garden types, like G. *cinereum, farreri,* and *dalmaticum,* to the robust G.
armenum, which will make a mound of greenery three feet tall, covered in fiercely
magenta flowers two inches across. Though the alpine Geraniums need sun and
well-drained soil, most others are easy to please, and will grow in sun or partial
shade. Some like the "Mourning Widow", (G. *phaeum*), have small, dark flowers,
but others, such as the pink G. *endressii,* and the blue G. 'Johnson's Blue' are
outstandingly bright. Many have intricate petal markings; none more so than the

little hybrid I introduced and named 'Ballerina', which has become very popular, though this is partly because it flowers for such a long time.

This — and a few other plants I have introduced — came as a bonus, with little effort on my part. Having a wide variety increases the chance of a natural break or improvement from self-sown seeds, and the only credit I can claim is that of spotting it and realizing its value. 'Ballerina' has saucer-shaped flowers, an inch across, of a lilac pink shade, delicately laced with purple markings. Seed saved from it produced another, also grey-leaved and four inches high, which I named 'Apple Blossom' in keeping with its colour, and shape.

I am not the only gardener to have sufficient liking for Grasses to set about collecting those with decorative qualities. My memory goes back to a time when my father used to cut a wild grass, (Deschampsia *speciosa*), growing in marshy spaces near the Ouse, both for home decoration and to send away to market on commission. For old times' sake I now have a garden group, as one of over fifty different kinds of perennial grasses — including sedges. Of the latter, Carex *morrowi* 'aurea variegata' is a splendid subject, with dense, brightly-striped foliage throughout the year. The outer blades bend over until they almost touch the ground, to give a charming mounded effect about twelve inches high, and it seems to flourish in almost any soil and situation. Molina *caerulea* 'variegata' likes it on the damp side, and this has flowers on airy two-foot stems, as well as good foliage, though not evergreen. Nor are the Miscanthus, which grow robustly but not invasively, from 3½ feet to nine feet high — in the case of M. *sacchariflorus.* This will make a good summer windbreak or provide rustling shade, but under M. *sinensis* there are three good garden subjects. M. S. 'gracillimus' is gracefully green to about 3½ feet, and M. S. 'zebrinus' has bars of gold across the long blades. M. S. 'variegatus' is spectacularly marked and showy from April to November, at about four feet. These seldom flower with me, but the green-leaved German variety 'Silver Feather' does in autumn, with six foot plumes.

The Germans must be more appreciative of the garden value of grasses, for most catalogues contain a wide selection. Judging from the greater number of firms specializing in Hardy Perennials it points to keen interest on the part of German gardeners than in England. They use grasses both in with flowering plants, and as ground coverers, and once when I called at a nursery near Darmstadt they were preparing an order for forty thousand Festuca *ovina* 'glauca'; a tufty, greyish, evergreen grass; for a war graves cemetery. The first time I visited this nursery, belonging to Karl Seibert, was in 1952. Then he was still struggling to restore what had been a fine nursery before the war, after its use from 1945 to 1950 as part of a U.S. Army training ground for tanks. Karl Foerster of Potsdam, the most famous of all German nurserymen, published a book in 1957 devoted entirely to grasses and ferns. I fancy he was the pioneer, by collecting, trying out and introducing those of decorative value, and he was still active when past ninety years old.

CHAPTER EIGHT

Hosta, Helleborus . . . .

THE HOE is one of the most rewarding of hand tools. This statement needs qualifying, of course, because hoeing outdoors between October and March is seldom possible. To be effective the soil surface needs to be reasonably dry, so that the hoe cuts cleanly, leaving no sticky soil on its bright steel blade. Under these conditions hoeing does good whether or not the ground is weedy, because it creates a tilth and helps capillary action. A crusty surface — liable to occur when heavy soil dries out — may be the result of panning when wet, and failing to stir it soon enough, and can bring the hoer aching arms and back. But for anyone who has succeeded in working in with the elements there is no pleasanter task than hoeing. Many a time when feeling frustrated, when fed up, careworn or even when angry, I've taken a hoe and vented my spleen on weeds, slicing them off as if they were the cause of my grievance. To see them wilting under sun and wind was like sweet revenge, and to free plants or whatever from their robbing, choking influence has brought back peace of mind.

To use weedkiller does not have this effect, though one must admit its value in places where it can kill only weeds. Nor do I care for mechanical hoers in a garden — not that these can be used except where plants or vegetables are grown in rows. Where they can be used the soil is liable to be left too loose and uneven, and some weeds half-buried will often take root again. Maybe they get over more ground in less time than hand hoeing, but apart from being hard to guide and turn machines cannot work so close to planted rows as can a hoe, if weeds are the reason for the exercise.

There are some garden plants which do not need hoeing round once they are established. These include nearly all Hostas which in spite of losing their foliage during the dormant winter period produce the kind of leaf cover over their rooting area in the growing season which will smother all annual weeds. Their root system is such that they can master most perennial weeds as well. Once planted they can stay for years, and although eighteen years is the longest I have allowed any to remain untouched in my garden, I'm pretty certain these would have continued to flourish for another eighteen, with the occasional mulching to keep them happy. On one occasion I had to dig down below where some four-year-old plants had grown and found their roots had penetrated for five feet into the stiff yellow clay below.

Hostas grow best where their ranging roots can find moisture and the richer the soil the more luxuriantly they grow, yet they are amazingly adaptable. All will grow in shade where not deprived of moisture, and these conditions are certainly best for the many with variegated leaves, because strong sun and dry wind scorches them. The one with the largest leaves, H. *sieboldiana* 'Elegans', will in time occupy a space a yard or more across, with bluish-green rounded leaves over a foot across, reaching out and up to 2½ feet or so. The lily-like flowers on spikes a foot or more taller, come in July and August, faintly lilac in colour. Even taller is the deep-green-leaved H. *rectifolia,* to which the name 'Tall Boy' is sometimes attached. This flowers very profusely—lavender mauve—on stems over four feet high, and with leaves most of the way up the stem as well. H. *ventricosa* too flowers well, with green leaves. So does H. *v.* 'Variegata', with the added attraction of a golden streak on each leaf.

At long last this valuable genus is receiving the popularity it deserves. In the pre-war years, as a nurseryman, I grew none for sale, for there was no apparent demand. It is the trend towards an appreciation for foliage as being complementary to flowers which has brought the hosta back into nurseries and gardens. Taste seems to have veered away, maybe for this reason, from subjects which make a blaze of colour for a long time, only to look shabby once fading sets in. The interest in Hostas has also caused controversy amongst the taxonomists. Nomenclature specialists in different countries have come out with their own findings as to which were the correct names for the many species in existence. Arguments ensued when one learned paper or treatise was in conflict with the statements made in another, and no final authority existed which could adjudicate.

This seems to be an insoluble problem affecting plant names. There is an international organization, but any decisions it makes when convened are seldom unanimous, nor are they binding on member countries. Certain rules and principles are, even if accepted by the majority, liable to be undermined. One of these is that the correct or paramount name of a species must be that given at its first recording, with total disregard of common usage. Thus, as the mass of data recorded but unpublished resting in the archives of the many botanical institutes came to be sorted, a good many instances of earlier specific names being given priority to later ones took places. One can imagine the delight it was to some back-room-boy on research, to discover, for example, the well-accepted Nepeta *mussinii,* (Catmint) should be dropped in favour of N. *faasenii,* because the latter was recorded a generation earlier. In addition to this kind of thing, is the work being continually carried on by taxonomists or classifiers. This results in merging, but more often sub-dividing groups of subjects, often giving new generic names to what were previously species of a genus. One easy example of many is of the Pasque Flower, well known as anemone *pulsatilla,* until given generic status as Pulsatilla *vulgaris.* Much more complicated and difficult to follow is when certain well-known Orchis are arbitrarily changed to the generic name of Dactylorrhiza, or the Oat grass species of Avena *candida* changed to Helichtrotrion *speciosum*. And there is no guarantee that such changes in nomenclature will be permanent.

But in coming back to Hostas, which for generations were named Funkias, there now seems to be a hope of their names being more stable. A few years ago, when attempting to come to adopt the correct names of those I grew, I came across some carrying three or four synonyms, with no reliable guides as to which to use. The muddle arose, one assumes, through various authorities registering them during the period when the Far East was a fruitful area for plant hunters, with little or no collaboration, until a century or so later the records had to be sorted out. Oddly, Hostas were rather neglected for a long period before about 1950, but evidence exists that they were widely used in Victorian times, since the variety 'Thomas Hogg' was raised well over a century ago. This has rounded leaves, with a marginal variegation, and is one of those best in shade. The nearest to it in appearance is a species name H. *crispula,* and during my sorting out period I was told by a visitor of repute as a Hosta specialist that the group I had labelled as H. *crispula* was in fact 'Thomas Hogg'. So in deference I changed the labels over, only to be told on his next visit, two years later, that my labels were in error. He'd forgotten his previous dictum, and being the kind of man who might deny having made it, I made no comment — but merely changed the labels over once more.

Of the thirty or forty different Hostas in my garden, the two smallest are the last to flower. One is H. *tardiflora,* growing only six inches high, with dark green leaves and lavender-mauve flowers, and H. *minor* 'alba', of similar height, but white. As with most other subjects that seldom come true from seed, there are those on the look-out for crosses and variations to launch as new and improved varieties. One of these to be recommended is the white-flowered and perfumed 'Royal Standard', green-leaved and statuesque at a good three feet. Others are on the way, including a cross between the bluish-leaved H. *sieboldiana* and the diminutive H. *tardiflora,* to which Eric Smith, its raiser, has given the name H. *tardiana.*

Although I have never found a self-sown seedling in my garden from a Hosta, capable as they are of interbreeding, Helleborus are quite promiscuous in this direction. The best known is of course the Christmas Rose, H. *niger* — which specific name obviously does not refer to its white flowers. In my experience, H. *niger* scarcely ever comes into flower for Christmas, and although it may if cloched, there remains a mystery unsolved. It is just possible that in its native lands of South and East Europe it habitually flowered at Christmas, but it has, over the four centuries since its introduction to Britain, adapted itself to a different climate. Another possibility is that with seed being the usual means of increase, its original flowering period has become, as it were, outbred.

Although it is of no vital importance, since by flowering from January to March it loses nothing of its cheer and value, there is one more puzzling aspect. Two or three people have, over the years, sent me plants which they aver regularly flower

Lining out seedling Helleborus—Christmas Rose.

in their gardens—widely separated—at Christmas. These I have planted hopefully, only to find that they are no earlier to flower than those I had already. So the mystery remains unsolved, and made more difficult to solve by the lack of vigour in plants increased by division. I once fell for the quite expensive purchase of five hundred plants of a Dutch clone, reputed to be invariably out for Christmas. They had been increased by division, and to ensure purity of stock and taking the long view, I thought it would prove a good investment. With a little more division, a carefully-prepared bed of over a thousand was planted up at Bressingham, but they made scarcely any growth. New leaves failed to appear at all on many, and after three years, scarcely a plant remained alive, and never a flower was seen. After such an experience, I reverted to seed-raised plants, which were not lacking in vigour. Seed collected in early summer was sown outdoors a few weeks later, which germinated the following spring. As an annual procedure we then were able to stock up to 100,000 plants from yearlings to clumpy three-year-olds, all grown on peaty soil which held nicely to their roots, and a fine sight they were when in flower.

H. *niger* has been crossed with other winter-flowering Helleborus—deliberately and otherwise. By February others more akin to the Lenten Rose, H. *orientalis,* are coming into flower. In the mild January of 1975, seven or eight species of Helleborus and numerous crosses were flowering together; a very propitious and permissive occasion for more promiscuity, no doubt. Over the years, interbreeding

Young lined out Helleborus *niger*. About 100,000 were reared annually by this method before the arrival of mechanical planters.

has been so widespread that in some instances doubts are raised as to which can be identified with certainty as the true original. Colours as well as habits vary so much, and though some are very charming as hybrids, well worthy of selection, the fact that they are so slow to increase by division, as the only means of ensuring trueness, is a deterrent. Some of my seedling hybrids have evergreen leaves — a distinct mark in their favour, to add to the charm of their speckled flowers in white, pink and purplish-red shades. This delightful mixture forms the basis of what my firm now sells as H. *orientalis*, the true stock of which is said to be white, and virtually lost to cultivation. As a species the many variations in colour it now includes have lost most of their leaves by the time flower buds appear. In my estimation, this is a factor which detracts from the overall appearance of the plants, and I feel no shame in allowing the sale of plants which will retain life-long greenery to complement the flowers, despite their having other blood than H. *orientalis,* in them.

What can be said of all those Helleborus coming under the Lenten Rose umbrella, is that they are easier to grow, and more reliably perennial than any other species. They prefer some shade, and will grow under trees where not completely deprived of light and moisture, and will flower year after year without attention. Though as plants they take time to reach a size large enough to divide, they resent being divided far less than H. *niger,* especially if this takes place in early autumn — the best planting time for all Helleborus.

There are some plants which will not divide, even with a knife. Nearly forty years ago I found the newly-introduced Thalictrum *dipterocarpum* 'Hewitt's Double' to be one such. It was introduced as a startling novelty by George Phillips, then owner of Hewitt & Co., of Solihull, and as a nurseryman I had to purchase some with a view to working up a stock to sell. This was at Oakington, and having fussed it for a year with extra good soil and attention, I dug up the six plants, only to find they were no larger than when planted. Each consisted of one little nub of a crown, below which was a small spread of thin feeding roots. A journalist friend, who knew George Phillips, hinted confidentially that if planted deeply, or mounded up, the stem leaf axils might produce tiny bulbils which if grown on would produce saleable plants in time. But war came. The experiment was neglected, and the plants died. I tried again in 1950, but again the result was negative. Thalictrum 'Hewitt's Double' baffled and teased me, although I knew one or two other nurserymen had found the secret. It was the fact that just a few bulbils were to be found after a summer's mounding up of soil, peat or sand, that made me persist in trying to encourage more.

But after more disappointments, I decided on an experiment I'd not dared to attempt before. The crown bud was seldom larger than a kidney bean, and to use a knife on this would seem to be a lethal operation. But there was nothing else left to try, and to go the whole hog, I cut the tips from a few crowns, and then with a razor blade, slit the lower half down, reducing it to two, three, and four sections, each with a little fibrous root attached. These were bedded in a box of sandy peat, and kept in the warm under glass. A month later, minute signs of new growth appeared, and by late May they had grown large enough to plant out. When dug in autumn they were as strong as those which had not been tampered with. This, then, was the method, and I could scarcely blame those who, having found the secret, kept it to themselves. I too have discovered propagating methods for a few plants difficult to propagate, and have been very choosy whom I told. And though more than once I've been deliberately put off, and suffered loss by being told the wrong method, so far as I remember I've never done this to anyone else.

The parent of 'Hewitt's Double', T. *dipterocarpum* is usually raised from seed. But this is single-flowered, and though unable to stand erect with its miriads of mauve, yellow-centred flowers on four to five-foot stems, it has great charm. 'Hewitt's Double' is not so tall, but is much less vigorous, and sets no seed. It also needs a rich moist soil, preferably with some shade, to give of its best.

Examples of crossings between two species are not uncommon. Eric Smith's Hosta *tardiana* is one of them—H. *tardiflora* × H. *sieboldiana,* but inter-generic hybrids are rare, and once made the resultant "mule" will produce no seed. By sheer good luck Percy Piper raised one seedling here from a cross he made at my suggestion between a Heuchera and a Tiarella. This would have been impossible had they not belonged to the same Family or Natural Order, in this case

Saxifragacaea. The luck was that this one seedling combined many good qualities of both parents. My father had in fact begun the process in the early 1920s when he crossed Heuchera *sanguinea* and H. *brizoides*. It was from this hybrid race that modern Heucheras have evolved, and one of them was used as parent, with Tiarella *wherryi*. That one tiny seedling flowered after two years, and when proof came of its qualities I named it after my eldest daughter, Bridget. But as a bi-generic hybrid, it could not take either parent's generic name — nor be hyphenated, so it came out as "Heucherella". It took six years to work up sufficient stock, all from division, before there were enough to launch it as a novelty. And it is such by-products of the plantsman's life — the hopes, the excitement, that add more than a touch of spice to the patient work plant breeding demands.

Heuchera 'Bressingham' strain, raised by author and father.

Heucherella 'Bridget Bloom', a bi-generic hybrid, named after the author's eldest daughter.

CHAPTER NINE

Irrigation, Iris . . . .

IRRIGATION is to me a subject of peculiar fascination. So much of my working life has been spent in coping with the harmful effects of too much moisture in the soil, and in irrigating when soil is too dry for good growth. I've dug ditches and laid drains to be rid of excess water, and dug several wells, as well as trenches in which to lay pipes for irrigation. I have also experimented with sub-irrigation, in the belief that moisture applied where the roots of plants can find it is better than overhead watering which tends to pan the soil. An inch of loose, dry soil on the surface, known as tilth, but with adequate moisture below that, is ideal for good growth.

Sub-irrigation — by means of land drain pipes which can be filled with water when need be — has this effect. But it involves levelling problems in laying the pipes, so that water applied does not all run to one end, making the soil too wet, and leaving the higher end almost as dry as before. The larger the area to be so watered the more formidable the task, and although quite easy for smallish, level garden plots, these also lend themselves to trickle irrigation, which has much the same effect.

A length of special hose, with tiny holes at intervals allows a slow trickle to penetrate downwards into the soil without saturating the surface and can do a power of good in a dry time, without wasting water. But a hose is an awkward thing to place between plants in a bed of any size, and to move it every couple of hours or whatever into the next position can be quite tedious and time-consuming.

In making my garden, situated as it is on the dry side of Britain, I had to lay water pipes for each new bed. In two, designed for moisture-loving plants, drain pipes for sub-irrigation were laid before planting, but in practice I found that overhead watering had to be applied to these just the same. With hind-sight, I can see now that to water the whole six acres effectively I should have laid main and branches, so that each bed had its built-in spray jets, to make hose pipes unnecessary. But at the time money was not available for such an expensive outlay. As it was, standpipes were placed as strategically as possible, close to the ground, and ever since rotary sprinklers on the end of moveable rubber hoses have had to cover the whole garden. During a dry time this takes three days. Moving the sprinklers every two hours or so takes up to half an hour, so that nearly a quarter of two helpers' time is taken up.

The alpine plunge beds with irrigation at Bressingham for pot grown plants.

In total — especially in years like 1975, when irrigation continued with scarcely a break from April to September — it would have easily paid the cost of fixed sprays at the outset.

During 1975 the garden was rather like an oasis, surrounded by the parched, unwatered meadow. Having three artesian boreholes, each up to two hundred feet deep into the chalk, has been more than a boon, supplying as they do the even more vital needs of the nursery. The watercourses in the chalk are trapped by an overlay of clay up to a hundred feet thick, but when this is punctured the water rises almost to the surface, and sometimes has to be capped to prevent it running to waste. Since childhood days it has always grieved me to see plants suffering from lack of moisture. Memories go back to when I used to help my father to cart water nearly two miles from the river, because the village pumps, ponds and wells, including his own, had dried up. And in spite of having had frustrations, hard work and losses from floods and waterloggings over many years, and in spite of knowing that too much water is more damaging than too little, summer rains are seldom unwelcome to me, even when not really in need of rain. So long as rain is gentle its effect is far more beneficial than that of irrigation. And to wander in a garden after a good rain following a dry spell is one of the sweetest experiences I know.

Some visitors have said what a joy it must be for me to sit down and survey the garden I've made. In one sense I can take it as the compliment intended, but I've never been able — nor have I had the wish — to indulge in that way. It has always been a joy, but not from any complacently prideful point of view. The grateful pleasure for me still comes from doing something, even if it's only weeding or studying the merits of certain plants in flower. If I were to stand or sit and stare, any thoughts of "this is my creation", if they occurred, would be dispelled by the awareness of a job in need of doing, or of some improvement that could be made. Perhaps with increasing age bringing decreasing zest or ability for work, I may be able to sit back and admire, but if I do, I hope it will be with thankfulness for having a variety of beauty at my doorstep — to absorb and appreciate — rather than of pride at being the one to place it there.

There are times, however, when I have found myself torn — wishing I had more time to stand and stare; to drink in the beauty of nature, believing that there's some truth in being "nearer to God's heart in a garden than anywhere else on Earth". Every spring has brought me an upsurge of emotion at the sight of the first flowers — Daffodils especially. But the period when Daffodils are in flower is invariably the busiest of the whole year, and with the rush still on their fading gives gives me a twinge, as I realize that for weeks I've been too preoccupied to absorb the wonder and beauty of spring as I'd hoped when its first signs appeared. It's the same with such scents as that of Lily of the Valley and of Honeysuckle, coming as they do, rather fleetingly, before summer has fully arrived. And when June slips by too, with the promise of spring bursting into high summer, I suddenly become aware that blackbirds too have ceased their song. The sights, smells and sounds of spring and early summer, to which I'd looked forward so much over the more dreary winter months, have passed with all too scanty appreciation from within myself. But this, I tell myself, is one of the penalties of being a nurseryman as well as a plantsman and gardener. Were it not for having to spend time on propagating and tending plants in rows, rather than in purely decorative groups, there would be more time in which to appreciate beauty. Maybe I would, but dyed in the wool as I am after a lifetime handling plants in quantity as well as variety, I doubt if I could ever resist continuing to do just that, whilst my physical activity remains.

It is probably true to say that a person's indolence and indifference will exact a price in many walks of life. They certainly will in one's attitude to gardening. But conversely industry and ingenuity on the part of a gardener shows up not only in the sight of a well-kept garden, but from the means its owner has used to work in with nature. If his interest stems from a love of the soil and what it will grow, it will be much more pleasing than if he merely keeps it tidy as a duty — like cleaning his car or shoes. A delight in gardening is much more likely to be generated by sowing a packet of seeds or planting an acorn and watching them grow than by having to keep up appearances for fear of what the neighbours might think.

All enthusiastic gardeners will have heard some people say that they can appreciate a good garden, whilst admitting they are not gardeners themselves, and regard any form of gardening as a chore to be avoided. Having heard some such remark, I have often wondered whether such people could be stimulated in some way to find the beginnings of a real interest. The thought has come partly because I find it difficult to understand how gardening can fail to appeal, and partly from regret that by having no interest they are missing out on one of the good things in life. It is one of the best of all antidotes to the harmful effects of the pace of living into which urban civilization and industrialization has forced us.

But there, I write as a countryman with ample garden space, and must remember that there are countless would-be gardeners living in towns and cities, perhaps in high-rise blocks, who have no chance to indulge in cultivating anything other than a few house plants. Such people can of course visit parks and gardens, and I daresay some are amongst the 150,000 or so who come each year to see mine, on Thursday and Sunday afternoons from May to October.

An open day — with traction engine rally in 1966. Taken from roof of Bressingham Hall.

Ivan J. Underwood

One source of pride to me, in which I feel no shame, is that there are certain plants to be seen here which visitors are unlikely to see anywhere else. Maybe any collector, no matter what his or her speciality, will feel this kind of pride, but having rare kinds of plants is rather different to having rare postage stamps or coins, because they are alive and capable of being increased in their own kind.

In this sense a gardener has an advantage as a collector, but is perhaps at some disadvantage if one's garden is open to public view. Plants need tending and watering; weeds must be kept down; the wear on grass paths made good, and watchful eyes kept on potential pilferers. Some of the latter seem to think that there's pride rather than shame to be gained by undetected pilfering of plants, seeds or cuttings. It is in fact just as wrong and antisocial as any other form of stealing, from shop-lifting to burglary. Although it very seldom occurs in my garden, on the few occasions it has I have come down hard on the offenders, who have been made to look very foolish in the eyes of other visitors who gathered round, who took the view that a privilege had been abused. There can never be a reasonable or valid excuse for anyone, no matter how keen they may be themselves as collectors, for indulging in mean, degrading pilferage in other people's gardens.

As a collector, Iris have not greatly appealed to me, and visitors will not see very many kinds in my garden. One reason for this could be that most kinds are so briefly in flower that they could easily be missed. This is true of the most popular breed of Iris—the June flowering I. *germanica,* with their huge and florid flowers seen in such a bewildering range of colour. Their popularity has I think dwindled somewhat, at least in England, and specialist nurserymen have dwindled. There are too many named varieties in existence for anyone to keep pace. Many have come from the U.S.A., where the Iris Society have been known to register over five hundred names of new varieties introduced in a single year. The Americans are equally exuberant with Hemerocallis, but at least these last much longer in flower than Iris, and unlike Iris are not prone to rhizome rot, which no doubt stems from crossbreeding and intensive propagation.

I have but a few groups of these large-flowered Iris, gorgeous though they are for about a fortnight. I also grow some species which do not stand out for colour but flower for a much longer period. One of these is I. *graminea.* Its leaves, as the name indicates, are broadly grassy, about ten inches tall, but the purplish flowers nestle within from May to July, not very noticeable, but from them comes the scent of ripe greengages. I. *innominata* makes much more of a show in a variety of shades and colours at about nine inches, rising above deep green leaves. On neutral or acid soil plants expand slowly and remain healthy for several years, and are easily raised from seed. Two other, taller species, easy to grow and a joy to behold are the light blues of I. *missouriensis* and I. *beesiana.* These are for early summer, but for winter cheer I. *stylosa* (*unguicularis*), especially planted against a wall, stands supreme.

CHAPTER TEN

Kniphofia, Koreans . . . .

I CAN just remember hearing that the botanic name for "Red Hot Poker" should be changed from Tritoma to Kniphofia. But after over fifty years one still sometimes hears the old name, and it just goes to show how once a name has become accepted there is a built-in resistance to change by almost everyone but the purists. Those of us who believe that the claims of common unage should take precedence over the findings of those dealing with names on an academic rather than practical basis, are likely to continue to resist changes which complicate, confuse and confound. But if Kniphofia has not been so difficult to swallow as some, I cannot help reflecting that if more time were spent on research into plant health and less on classification, it would be of infinetely wider benefit. Kniphofias are suffering from a peculiar disease, capable of turning a hitherto robust clump into a rotting mass at just below ground level. Perhaps the experts are already working on it, following trials begun at Wisley Gardens in 1974 which ended as a fiasco. These scheduled trials are always interesting, and often helpful. Anyone can enter by sending a few plants of a species or variety at a given time, after filling in the requisite forms, With large numbers of both cultivators and species in cultivation, the R.H.S. endeavour to attract a wide variety, and grow them on to be judged by a Trials Committee. Although I have had to resist becoming a member of the Committee, I can and do support it by entering plants for trial most years. For the Kniphofia Trials I sent about a dozen kinds, some of which were new ones I had raised over the past few years.

Although I was bothered about the crown rot disease which had affected some older cultivatars, those new ones I sent appeared to be perfectly healthy. But it came as a shock to learn in the early summer of 1974 that the Kniphofia Trials had been cancelled, and the whole lot dug up and burned. I imagine there would have been about forty kinds or more in the Trial, and though the decision to scrap it was doubtless taken with the best of motives, those who contributed to it are still in the dark as to the nature of the disease, much more its cure or prevention. We must assume it to be a soil-borne virus, and I would not be the only one to know that it has been in existence for well over twenty years.

Its symptoms are foliage collapsing and rotting at the base during summer, which gradually affects the whole plant. Resurgent growth sometimes appears in the following year, and though a stock is often decimated, some plants remain unaffected. Some kinds appear to be immune, including those that make woody

◁ Interior of the first propagating glasshouse, built in 1948.

growth above ground, like a Yucca, and any plants raised from seed. In general it is the older varieties that are most liable, and I could name a few which now seem to be extinct, probably for this reason. Kniphofias are such decorative plants, and it is a pity people should be deterred from growing them for lack of co-ordinated research for the cause and cure of this disease, which seems to wax and wane in cycles over the years.

About 1960 I obtained three plants of the rare K. *erecta*. Its tubular, scarlet flowers hang down at first, like any other, but as they open fully they then face mouth upwards — hence the name "erecta". It is said to be of unknown garden origin. As it was a distinctive rarity I set about building up a stock by division. It took ten years, and just when there were sufficient to offer, the rot set in, and I'm back to about fifty plants, all of which appear to be perfectly healthy. This pattern has occurred with others, including the charming ivory-coloured 'Maid of Orleans', and the massive, six-foot orange-scarlet 'Samuel's Sensation'.

A lady approached me on an Open Day, when I was waiting for my little train to fill up with passengers, for which I was engine driver on the Nursery Line.

"I was glad," she said with some diffidence, "to see Kniphofia *galpinii* in your garden, because it was my father, Dr Galpin, who first found it growing wild in South Africa". There was just time to tell her that I prized it — especially after working up a stock of over two thousand, only to lose all but the garden group of a dozen, during the winter of 1963.

From K. *galpinii*, which is orange-flowered, dwarf and very late-flowering, we were once able to save some seed. By the long process of selection, four varieties were named — with 'Bressingham' as prefix. Two were twice as tall as the parent, but with the same grassy foliage, and they flowered two months earlier. Two more, 'Comet', and 'Gleam', were even more colourful, but these were almost as late and scarcely any taller than the eighteen-inch K. *galpinii*.

I fancy there must be some *galpinii* blood in another new variety, raised by that gifted, enthusiastic specialist Beth Chatto. It is named 'Little Maid', and is indeed a little treasure, with all the charm in miniature of the ivory-primrose coloured 'Maid of Orleans' — and it flowers for weeks. There are probably about thirty true species of Kniphofia and more than this of named cultivars, not counting the infinite variations that appear when the latter are raised from seed.

Most references to Kirengeshoma *palmata*, however, state that it is a monotypic genus. Another distinction exists in the generic name which is, or was for a long time, the only one with its origin in the Japanese language. As a garden subject, it is not difficult in good soil, where not dry, with some shade. It grows bushily to about three feet, and has light yellow, waxy-textured flowers which droop without fully opening. If only they would reveal themselves more fully it would be a first class subject, for it flowers from July to October, and it just fails on this one count.

A year or two ago a note on Kirengeshoma *palmata* appeared in the R.H.S. journal. With a full description of its merits and requirements, it was again stated to be a monotypic genus. I was tempted to dispute this, because I possessed another, quite distant, species, named K. *koreana.* But because I had only half-a-dozen plants and had no record of where my original plant, from which they had been increased, had come from I decided to wait. I hoped someone else might come forward, and in the meantime, increase my stock, so as to be able to supply what I consider to be a more gracefully-erect subject, carrying its flowers in almost candelabra formation. So far it has set no seed, and increase by division is rather slow.

There can be no doubt as to the native habitat of Kirengeshoma *koreana* but this could scarcely be said of Korean Chrysanthemums. Not that one hears so much about them nowadays as was the case in the 1930s, when they were launched as novelties.

News of the existence of this new race of Hardy Chrysanthemums broke in about 1935. The firm W. Wells Jnr, of Merstham were specialists in both Hardy Plants and Chrysanthemums, and Ben Wells, the owner, had a range of Koreans on trial from the American firm Bristol Nurseries of Connecticut. Advance publicity in the horticultural press indicated that Wells had sole distribution rights in the U.K., but having exported some plants to the order of Bristol Nurseries early in 1937, I was later intrigued to receive an invitation from them to try out a range of their Koreans myself. It was almost too good to be true, for one who having taken the plunge in going in for wholesale only not long before, and steadily gaining business and confidence, I accepted gladly. There was a hint that Bristol Nurseries were somewhat peeved because Ben Wells had been tardy in launching their range.

Twenty-five rooted cuttings of each of eight varieties arrived in May, 1937, and five of each were planted up in a trial plot. The rest were propagated by Len Smith, (of whom more later), as hard as he knew how, till by autumn we had several hundred of each. Regardless of Ben Wells' intentions we had sufficient stock to justify a splurge, offering rooted cuttings the following spring. But Ben Wells, having learned that he had not got a clear field, sent me a letter expressing a grievance with Bristol Nurseries for allowing me to acquire stock, but also suggesting that if I would row in with him over pricing, he would allow me to book orders for several other varieties he had, which I had not. The upshot was a visit to Merstham. There I was taken out for lunch and shown his nursery, but when it came down to brass tacks, he would not give a guarantee I felt was needed. It was all very well to peg my prices to his, in return for being able to offer a wider range, but I wanted assurance that if I booked orders to varieties of which I had no stock, they would be met by him. Ben tried both pleading and bluster, but I would not give way, and returned home after an exciting day, determined once more to paddle my own canoe.

A folder was then printed showing my eight varieties in colour, photographed from the five plants of each which had been allowed to flower. It was enclosed in an issue of the weekly *Horticultural Trade Journal,* sent out to nearly 7,000 traders in the early spring of 1938, and despite the threat of war, orders came in with a rush, to reach a total value of about £1,500. It was this which enabled me to buy the farm in the Fens — two hundred acres for £1,600 — at Burwell. It also encouraged me to go in more strongly for Korean Chrysanthemums. My catalogue, sent out in the autumn of 1939, listed more varieties, but — as for the 1,868 other kinds of plants it offered — there was practically no sale. And by 1945, when the nursery slowly began to come back to life, there were no Korean Chrysanthemums left at all — nor have I grown any since.

There is a tail piece to add. Ben Wells also came out with an offer; more attractively pictured than mine. But his was a mainly retail business, and I could but imagine he suffered no great loss through me. The greatest loss was that his nursery never recovered from the results of war, which included his own death, presumed drowned on an Atlantic crossing, I believe, in 1943.

It was during the summer of that year when an invitation came from Fred Simpson of Otley to inspect some new Korean Chrysanthemums he had raised and wished to sell. I took it as a compliment, and though up to my neck at the time with the cares of the thirty-six acres at Oakington, and over five hundred acres at Burwell, twenty miles away, I decided to go. Having seen and admired his new range, I listened as Fred confided that he was a sick man, with not much time to live. They would, he assured me, be money-spinners to anyone able to give them the publicity they deserved, and he had given me first refusal. This touched me, but it needed careful thought. In keeping my promise to decide within a week, I found I had no stomach for what it would entail, with so much already on my plate. In suggesting Baker's of Wolverhampton, I knew that such a firm would give them the right treatment for maximum sales. Though Baker's also faded out after Jimmy Baker died, the Otley Koreans were, under his direction, given a splendid launching, just as had been staged for Russell Lupins and Symons Jeune Phlox.

CHAPTER ELEVEN

Liriope, Linum . . . .

LATHYRUS *odoratus* is the Latin name for Sweet Pea, and in a garden near Richmond, Yorkshire, Flora and I were once shown the original type from which all modern Sweet Peas have been evolved. Bobby James was proud of it, even though to almost anyone else it would appear as very inferior. But Bobby James was also proud, he said, of being a Victorian. At the time of our visit — about 1958 — he was well over eighty, and could therefore qualify as Victorian, though what he meant was that it was the old times, ways and attitudes that appealed most to him. This nostalgia did not prevent him from cracking jokes every few minutes as we wandered round a garden that would have been modern by the conventional Victorian standard. His liking for old-fashioned plants was almost a fervour, but his ebullience was infectious.

Bobby James was one of many enthusiastic gardeners we met on the swopping trips we made as my own garden grew, between 1958 and 1963. To be able to talk plants breaks down barriers which might otherwise exist to a formidable degree, and I can think of no garden visited where we were not welcomed. There were, however, one or two occasions when we feared we'd made a mistake, judging by first impressions. One of these was when we entered a dark canopy of trees over the drive leading to a large house, near Penrith. The house itself also appeared dark and rather forbidding under the threatening clouds, and the whole place seemed eerie and deserted. Hoping to find someone, Flora went one way, and I took another. But eventually the Torbock brothers spotted us and escorted us charmingly round their very interesting, if isolated garden.

We feared a chilly reception at Keillour Castle in Perthshire. Not having written, I telephoned the evening before from the hotel in Crieff, where we had decided to stay overnight, not daring to call on chance late in the day. Mrs Knox-Finlay answered, and with a somewhat reluctant "if you must" attitude gave permission to visit next morning. Her husband met us and we saw plants and talked plants for two hours or so before he invited us in for sherry. It was then that Mrs Knox-Finlay, to whom we were introduced, relaxed into a welcome, when told the name was Bloom, and not Groom, as she'd understood from my telephone call.

On a visit to Ireland we were invited to take lunch with Lord Talbot at Malahide Castle, which he and his sister occupied. The rather grim exterior was cosier inside, in spite of vast stone staircases and evidence of baronial fixtures, fittings and ancestry. The conversation was formal, as were the hovering manservants who served the meal, but once outside in the garden, the language of plantsmen took over. The rather austere owner showed us the large collection he had gathered together in quite recent years. But nothing was labelled. Instead, Lord Talbot explained queries from a large ledger-type of book, in which every subject was recorded, with its exact garden location—except for a few which had been unaccountably omitted, thereby causing a certain amount of consternation. It was however a collection of which he could be justly proud, and it was a loss to horticulture when he died long before it had fulfilled the plans he'd laid down for it.

One other encounter is worth recording. It was in Sweden in 1959; having spent a very interesting and rewarding day in the Botanic Garden at Gothenburg, we were advised to go to the Sofiero Gardens, near Helsingfors. We stayed the night at a nearby motel, and next morning turned the car into the back entrance to the garden, hoping we would be allowed in. I left the car in a lane, and on opening a door saw two men across a yard, intent on the contents of a frame. One of them came to meet me with an unwelcoming expression on his face. I made my request in English, but although his reply was in Swedish, which I could not understand, it was obvious that he was embarrassed. His tall companion had wandered farther on, but on noticing me, still trying to converse, with Flora nearby, he came over.

"Can I help?", he asked, speaking in perfect English. It was then that I knew who he was, and having told us where to park the car, King Gustav of Sweden spent the next two hours showing us the garden of his summer palace. It was such a rare privilege—and it filled us with admiration when, having excused himself because of an appointment, the eighty-year-old king waved back as he went out of sight, striding upwards along a steep path to the palace.

The late King Gustav was a botanist as well as a plantsman, and his erudition covered many other fields. He grew a wide selection of woodland plants, including Rhododendrons, Azaleas, Primulas and Lilies. My knowledge of these subjects has always been very scanty, and it was difficult to avoid showing my ignorance. It was in Sofiero that we saw the unusual and attractive parasitic plant, Lathraea *clandestina*—the Blue Toothwort. It grows on the damp roots of Poplar and Willow trees without any detrimental effect, and although the hooded purple flowers which come in spring are quite sizeable, they are practically stemless, at two-inches high. To get it established one has to dig down to find a main tree root and place a little clump on a bared portion before gently pulling back some fine moist soil around it.

For a long-flowering subject in poor, dry soil, Lavatera is a shrub without rival. The rosy pink saucers, 2 inches across, of L. *olbia* 'rosea' will begin opening in May and continue right through till November as the stems run up to a bushy six or seven feet. Such exuberance, as might be expected, is produced at the expense of longevity. In my garden there is a group which has been there for over twenty years, but only because I gap up every spring to replace any old plants which have become

A nursery field in the valley bottom.   *Michael Warren*

exhausted. It has been well worth the little trouble involved in taking a few cuttings in late summer, which root quite easily in a frame, and cutting the old plants hard back in March of all the previous year's growth. By May new shoots are running up and quickly break into flower, nestling amid the greyish-green leaves. It much prefers poor or stony soil to anything moist or rich, but given good drainage and a position in full sun it will flourish.

The Liriopes have suffered from undeserved neglect, especially L. *muscari*. I first saw this years ago in a botanic garden, relegated to a dry, shady position, where it was flowering but sparsely. But the spikes of light violet-purple, barely eighteen inches high, were attractive — tiny bells hugging the upper stem, as do Grape Hyacinth, rising above darkly evergreen, bladed foliage. Having acquired some plants, I placed some in shade and others in sun. The fibrous roots carried little storage globules, which seemed to indicate that it was drought-resistant. Both groups grew well, but those in full sun produced not only more growth of brighter green, but flowered much more freely than those in the shade. The flowers come in late summer and autumn, and as the plants need no attention for years, L. *muscari* is a splendid little subject, especially for those looking for trouble-freedom. Weeds stand little chance in a well-established group.

A leaflet once arrived, from a nurseryman in Texas, which featured a new hybrid Liriope named 'Majestic'. There was a colour picture of a long garden path with this as an edging on both sides, flowering even more profusely than L. *muscari*, but not so tall, and with broader leaves. I wrote to enquire the price, having decided we ought to have it, but instead of a letter in reply, a parcel containing twenty-five plants arrived by air about three months later. But there was no invoice, and even a letter asking for one produced no response of any kind. This took place about twelve years ago, and though a bill never came, L. 'Majestic' has never thrown any flowers of any significance. After one hot, dry summer a few appeared, but it evidently needs more sunshine than Norfolk can provide to make it flower well.

Liriopes are so closely related to Ophiopogons that confusion over nomenclature makes separation by ordinary folk impossible. For one of them the generic synonym of Convallaria is given, thus linking them to Lily of the Valley as well, under the vast and varied Liliacea family. Some Ophiopogons—or Liriopes—are at first glance more like a rhizome-creeping grass, and I've seen L. *gramnifolia* used extensively in Sorrento as a substitute for grass in parks and hotel gardens.

Under Ophiopogon *planiscapus* there is a dark green, grassy-looking plant, strongly evergreen, which creeps slowly below ground, giving it some value as ground cover in sun or shade. But a variation of this, with the indicative name 'nigrescens' is as near black-bladed as could be. Its tiny spikes flower at about four inches high with little by way of colour display, but nearly everyone falls for its arching black foliage and neat habit. It likes some shade and humus-rich soil, and is of Japanese origin. My original stock came from Mr Wada in Japan, and its popularity prompted me to procure some more, three years after the first consignment. But by then the price had shot up to ten times as much and I had to fall back on the slow process of dividing the few I had left, apart from the 25 per cent which came true from the small amount of seed it yields.

One needs to be careful when writing about plants, and when explaining the faults or virtues of any subject it is safest to add "in my experience". I once extolled Linum *narbonense* as possessing all it takes to be rated as first class. In the same book I faulted Salvia *haematoides* on the grounds that it was not long-lived. Both statements were made unequivocally, but a reader of my book, who lived near Manchester, took me to task. In his garden Linum *narbonense* seldom survived a second winter, and his plants of Salvia *haematoides* had flowered reliably without loss of vigour for nine years.

Maybe Lithospermum 'Heavenly Blue' is not long-lived in some gardens. In alkaline soil it virtually refuses to grow at all, but where it is happy it will give an intensely blue carpet of flowers for several weeks. This, with the later inclusion of the slightly larger-flowered variety 'Grace Ward' have been consistent best sellers for over fifty years — better than any other single colour rock garden plant I know. Some nurserymen able to propagate it with lime-free soil and water have for years produced many thousands annually with which to supply others who cannot grow it. Eventually all are sold to the gardening public, and no doubt their losses are frequent. But still the demand holds up, because its appeal is quite irresistible.

In the minds of some gardeners the name Flax makes them think of Flaxen or yellow hair. But the Linums include bright blue — as in the case of L. *narbonense*, already mentioned — and yellow. With the longer experience I now possess I would say that none are long-lived, and they are especially resentful of winter damp. Also in the mind, Lobelia as a name indicates blue, because the best known is the annual blue flowered type used for summer bedding and hanging baskets. But there are taller-growing Lobelias with bright red or pink flowers. One of these is L. *cardinalis,* with leafy spikes of lipped, scarlet flowers. It grows wild beside streams in the bleak New England and Middle West of the U.S.A., where winter temperatures fall well below those in the U.K. Yet in Britain it will seldom winter outside, and if through being protected it survives, it is unlikely to recover from a second flowering. The reason, one can only suppose, it that L. *cardinalis* is accustomed, in the wild, to drier winters, which if harsh, provide regular snow cover.

I have given up struggling to grow both Lobelia *cardinalis,* and the hydrids which go under the specific name of *fulgens.* The latter include some very showy ones, and the purple-leaved, crimson-flowered 'Queen Victoria' is still used extensively for bedding. The finest I ever grew was 'Bees Flame', which produced large spikes up to three feet, until gradually it lost vigour and faded out. Perhaps I took too little care and trouble, preferring to leave plants out over winter, protected with litter, rather than lift and frame them each autumn. I followed the latter practice for a year or two, but losses were heavy. My only excuse for allowing such showy subjects to disappear from the garden is that of being a specialist in hardy perennials. The fact is that the effort to save them calls for both careful timing and much fussing — unlike some of the other tender subjects I grow, such as Penstemons, from which a few autumn cuttings can so easily be taken to make good any winter losses.

The Lythrums must surely rank as the hardiest and most adaptable of perennials. The native Purple Loosetrife, Lythrum *salicaria,* grows naturally in damp places. Whether in sun or shade its slender spikes, rising on branching, twiggy stems from a hard, woody rootstock will grace a garden too. Richer colours in such improvements as 'The Beacon' and 'Robert' will also grow practically wherever they may be planted, in any kind of soil, though naturally the better the soil, especially if damp, the happier they will be, and the longer their display. To carve up an old plant needs a chopper rather than a knife. But I discovered by accident an easier means of propagation from cuttings. The spring shoots are fairly easy to root in any case, given warmth, but when 'The Beacon' first came out in the 1930s the dozen plants I bought for stock were placed in a box under glass so as to hasten new growth for propagating. Through an oversight it was left untouched for several weeks, and the shoots were a foot or more tall. Instead of using just a three-inch tip as the only cuttings, each stem was sectioned to make four or five, and each section took root as readily as the tips, so that twelve plants made several hundreds more within the year.

The Yellow Loosestrife is Lysimachia *punctata* (or *vulgaris*), but I fell for a rosy-red species, some years ago, named L. *leschenaultii* with glowing spikes 12-18 inches tall. It had been given an Award of Merit as a hardy plant in 1932, which I believed was well-deserved, until I found that this too disliked our damp winters. It was sad to see the stock dwindling, but even my garden group became steadily thinner, and failed to produce either seed or cuttings to keep it going. Now, it remains but a memory of a very attractive little plant that is no more. Perhaps it still exists in some more favoured garden than mine. Or maybe it has joined the ranks of subjects which despite their A.M., R.H.S., have failed to stand the more vital judgement of climate. Perhaps it was expecting too much, since its native home is in the Nilghiri Hills of India.

CHAPTER TWELVE

Mulching, Mustard . . . .

MULCHING as an aid to good gardening is being increasingly practised. Its triple benefits come from better growth because the soil beneath it is less liable to dry out and breathes more freely; from a gradual build-up of humus content in the soil; and from keeping weeds at bay. For some years past I have been using compost spread over such subjects as Astilbes, Hostas and Phlox, with good results except for the weeds that lurk as seeds in the mixture. On groups of quite dwarf kinds — autumn Gentians, Polygala *chamaebuxus,* Ericas and dwarf Azaleas, peat has been used effectively, making me wish I could cover the whole garden with a weed-free mulch. During 1974, when such constant watering was necessary, that wish bit deeply, especially after seeing Beth Chatto's delightful garden near Colchester. She had mulched several large beds with coarse peat, and her plants were flourishing in spite of drought and in spite of no overhead irrigation.

The resolve I must try hard to carry out is to use compost for digging in and to confine its use as a mulch to such as Hostas, with weed-smothering properties. But I am torn between using peat and another mulching substance which has more recently become available. This is pulverized bark, which the Forestry Commission prepares for horticultural use. It bears some resemblance to a coarse peat, and is said to be of similar nutrient value. Both are of course expendable from weathering, worms and shrinkage, but though bark has the appearance of being longer-lasting than peat, this factor remains to be proved. Two inches depth of either is about the maximum coating amongst erect-growing plants and shrubs, but a thinner one for smaller, bushy or very low-growing subjects, for which I fancy peat is still the best material. Such a dressing should keep down most weeds for two years and one has to decide what labour cost this would save, adding such saving to its benefit to plant-growth and the soil itself. A sum can only be reached on the basis of the time a mulch takes to apply, added to the cost of the material itself, and how long it lasts.

One certain thing is that a skimped dressing will prove less effective as a weed smotherer. Someone I know with a large garden in which shrubs predominate, has for years used lawn mowings as a mulch amongst them. Though he is well pleased with the result, I would find it too unsightly amongst perennials to consider it, though disposal of mowings from my garden has always been a nuisance and a problem. Another friend with an even larger garden — several acres of shrubs — uses a surface weedkiller spray. There are no weeds, but the arid appearance of bare ground is also unsightly.

On small patches of heavy clay soil I have used sand as a mulch, and found it effective in much the same way as peat. Since sand is not expendable it makes heavy soil easier to work, and more porous as it becomes mixed in. By way of contrast and by the way, I have used clay to give body to sandy peat soil. Ten acres of the fen fields at Bressingham were treated in this way during the 1950s, not so much as a mulch, but as a covering to be mixed in by ploughing and rotavating to improve the top twelve inches—which it certainly did. But peat or pulverized bark are the dual-purpose mulches—soil improvers and weed-smotherers. If compost made from mainly garden refuse could be sterilized it would also be trouble-free. Mine includes farmyard muck from pigs, which if it enriches and rots more quickly, adds, if anything, to the weed seed content of the whole.

For the first year or two after carving out my island beds from old pasture neither fertility nor weeds were a problem. Apart from wind-borne seeds—like sow thistle and groundsel—most other weeds have come in from the compost and manure I've used to keep up fertility. We reckon to prevent weeds from seeding amongst plants by hoeing before they reach the seeding stage, but a few always escape by lurking unseen. It is said groundsel will reproduce up to six times in a year from a single seedling, whilst chickweed and annual nettle will shed seed all the year round. One year's seeding, they say, means seven years's weeding, and as this is largely true, there's much to be said for the outlay of weed-free mulch like peat and bark, and for resolving to rely more on these in future.

Helxine *soleirolii* is also known as "Mind your own Business". I planted some as an addition to my collection of plants in a dampish, shady place at the foot of a wall. At first the close, bright green, filmy carpet it made was quite pleasing, and though not reckoned to be 100 per cent hardy it survived the severe 1963 winter. Since then it has climbed up and spread along the wall, up some steps and into every crevice in brickwork and flint, and into the adjoining beds, in which some of my choicest plants grew. It has defied every effort made to eradicate it, whether by scraping with a tool or finger nails, and has even resisted an aerosol weedkiller spray. It wandered into a group of the creeping Phlox *adsurgens* which I treasured, and in desperation I had to painstakingly dig up the lot to save it from being choked to death. Just opposite there was a patch of the tiny creeping mint, Mentha *requinii*, which has a very similar habit of growth. But it is not the habit of Helxine *soleirolii* to mind its own business by keeping itself to itself. Instead it became so invasive that separation from the Mentha was quite impossible. In fact they were so alike that to be sure of which was which I had to rub my fingers over the green mat and decide from the minty odour this produced.

It was close by this spot that in making a little stream bed with concrete, I unknowingly introduced another plant which became a weed. Taking an easy way, through shortage of time, I asked one of our customers to send a collection of suitable subjects for a shallow stream, since they were specialists in aquatics.

Garden making, 1958.

Amongst the four or five kinds they sent was one with the interesting name of Veronica *beccabunga*. As a name it was unfamiliar, but as a plant I had a vague impression of having seen it, or something very like it, growing wild. It very soon grew wild in and beside that trickle of a stream. This too has defied complete eradication, for unlike the Helxine it produces both flower and seed, and I soon discovered that Veronica *beccabunga* was in fact the weed growing in our fen ditches, so abundantly that I'd never bothered to notice it sufficiently to look up its name — better known perhaps as "Brooklime".

I suppose I should be ashamed to admit that I have tended to ignore native plants, taking no trouble to identify more than a few that were out of the ordinary. Maybe this comes from the nurseryman background, but it has often been a surprise to come across, in parts of the Waveney Valley fens bordering Bressingham, several which have links, at least, with subjects grown as nursery or garden plants. Several hundred acres of quite wild fen lie at this upper end of the valley. There is a road running north and south three miles from here, where at one point there is a ditch on either side. One is the source of the Little Ouse, flowing west, whilst opposite is the Waveney, flowing east. It is here that the area known as Redgrave Fen is now a Wildlife Trust, and is becoming well known for its rich native flora. Amongst the many grasses Molinia *caerulea* can be found, but I did not notice it enough to realize that from this came the variegated-leaved form which I'd been growing for years. The green type is scarcely garden-worthy, but Molinia *caerulea*

Groups of shade-loving plants.

'variegata' certainly is. Its soft, narrow blades are renewed every spring to make a cascade of bright foliage about twelve inches high, and above these comes a hazy mass of tiny, brown flowers on slender sprays during summer. It grows best in damp, sandy or peaty soils, or otherwise good garden soil which is not too dry, where it will form non-invasive, trouble-free clumps.

I tried, but failed to succeed, with Mertensia *pterocarpa*. Knowing that most Mertensias preferred some shade and a cool, leafy soil, I planted my original stock in what should have been a perfect site, and was entranced to see the little waxy bells of shy blue, dangling above the blue-grey pointed leaves. But the following spring five of the ten plants had rotted away, and although I managed to knife the two largest remaining into four, they showed their resentment of such treatment by sulking, and death claimed them when winter came. After three years none were left alive, and I was left with no alternative but to add this to my failures. But two years later, having by then something else in the space it had occupied, I spotted a tiny seedling, its one developing leaf reminding me of the dear departed. With due fussing it grew, and when it flowered the next year it was M. *pterocarpa* — with a difference. It was slightly taller, at about eight inches, but more leafy, vigorous and compact, and it carried bells of glistening light blue for much longer, from early June to late August. Somehow a natural hybrid had occurred, and I was delighted when, after two years, it broke naturally into three as my fingers prised apart its black fleshy roots. Eventually, when this process every spring brought the stock up to a couple of hundred, I named it 'Blue Drop' for want of anything better, and although it has shown distress in wet soil, it will grow in open as well as shady positions.

Mertensia *virginica* — Virginian Cowslip.

Those who prefer showy, flamboyant subjects might not be impressed with the demure beauty of M. 'Blue Drop', much less the little carpeting species M. *primuloides*, with small, deep blue flowers. But I cannot imagine anyone not admiring M. *virginica*, the Virginian Cowslip. The purplish shoots push through in early spring, and gradually unfurl, taking on a lighter shade, freshly glaucous, and then the flowering stems reach up and out to nearly two feet, dangling with bells of waxy sky blue, which take on a faint tinge of pink as they fade, late in May. It is a uniquely beautiful plant, a perfect companion for such as Dicentra *spectabilis,* the "Bleeding Heart". Like this, it has an ugly fleshy root, black and brittle, to which, unfortunately, it dies back completely by July. But it's worth marking the spot where it rests, to avoid risk of damage when digging or hoeing.

The brave sight of a field of mustard in flower is not so often seen as once it was. Nowadays farmers seem less concerned with such crops known as "bastard fallows", to plough in for soil improvement. Although mustard ploughed in when at maximum growth during summer was most often used, buckwheat and rape were also grown. They not only added nitrogen to the soil, but improved its structure as well. What is more , mustard has been known to choke and kill some perennial weeds, such as creeping cress and sorrel, which can be more than a nuisance in acid soils. Both can become a menace in a garden also, but any garden plot will be improved by digging in "green manure" as mustard and the like are sometimes termed. Only a little preparation is needed so as to scatter the seed, which is cheap to buy. It is then raked in, and at any time between April and October, will germinate and grow so quickly that in a matter of weeks it is in flower. Where poor and dry it may reach only a foot or two, and neither water nor fertilizer would be wasted to help it run up to twice that height and to thicken out. Then when it is fully developed, a garden roller, or even stamping, will flatten it ready for digging.

Upon reflection, I've had quite a lot to do with mustard during my lifetime. It began when I was a small boy, for my father grew both mustard and cress under glass each year from Christmas to Whitsun, as a salad crop. My first experience in business, at about eight years old, was to take it round the village to sell at a penny a bag. These bags were the then 4oz. sweet bags, and for years my father always cut the mustard first, to go in the bottom, and then filled the bag almost to overflowing with cress, with the skilful use of a sharp dinner knife. My commission was a penny in the shilling, and remained so even when, during the 1914-18 war, the price went up to 1½d per bag. But by the time I was fourteen my father handed that side of his business over to me, though often enough he had to help me with the sowing and the cutting. Nowadays, mustard is often sold on its own as mustard and cress, but the latter is less hot to the tongue, and has smaller, divided leaves of a brighter green.

Mustard also played an important part in my life as a farmer, twenty years or so later. Many Fen farmers grew mustard for seed, mostly on contract to Colmans. Sown in early May, it was ready for harvesting just after the corn harvest was ended, cut usually by an old-fashioned sail-reaper and carted loose. There came a time when, having reclaimed derelict land from its reeds and bushes, a smother crop was needed before normal crops could be grown. Mustard was one obvious choice, and by 1943, when I and my helpers had cleared and ploughed over two hundred acres of the wild fen, half was put down to mustard for seed. Such peaty soil did not need it to be ploughed in as green manure, and by leaving it for seed the maximum smotherage of native weeds was achieved. But if the yield was quite good and the desired results for the soil satisfactory, the price of seed was pretty low. Food shortages were not made good by the copious use of mustard, and Colmans wanted nothing to do with the forty tons of seed for grinding that came from my hundred-acre crop.

Buckwheat was also used as a smother crop. It was just as effective, and the seed, being of quite good food value for both animals and humans, was in much greater demand. But it was tricky stuff to harvest, especially in a damp season, as it was in 1942, when I had well over a hundred acres of it. Neither stems nor leaves nor seed would dry off and harden, and it flopped weakly, making even the old soil-reaper clog up. All but one field of thirty acres was at last cut and carted, but by then it was late October, and still damp, for this field had been late sown owing to its dense covering of bushes having first to be cleared. This had taken a gang of nearly twenty men, and as most of them were still my helpers, sixteen of them able to use a scythe were set to work mowing by hand. I could not resist joining them, and in two or three days it was done. It was a rare sight, those sixteen men swinging scythes, one behind the other, and I learned more of what I needed to know to keep up with them. But as an exercise it was doomed. The resultant stacks rotted, in spite of being thatched and aired, and did not yield enough seed to cover the cost of harvesting.

CHAPTER THIRTEEN

Nepeta, Orchis . . . .

AMONGST the most widely-used hardy plants over the past fifty years Nepeta has been outstanding. I refer of course to the Catmint known for so long as Nepeta *mussinii,* but now said to be correct as N. *faassenii*—a name unlikely to become generally accepted by gardeners. So far as my memory goes it sprang into popularity in the early 1920s, for I went to learn and work on Wallace's Nursery at Tunbridge Wells in 1923, and soon heard about the phenomenal demand there was for it. At the staff concert the firm held someone parodied the then popular song, "Yes, We Have No Bananas", with "Yes, We Have No Nepeta", with the rest of the lines in keeping with the fact that the demand was far in excess of supply. With such a plant capable of rapid increase, growers, including my father soon afterwards, saw to it that the demand was met. Countless thousands were produced annually, and still are. It is what producers call "a good nurseryman's plant". It is cheap to produce and sells pretty consistently as a subject for edging and bedding, flowering as it does for months. But winter losses—through exhaustion and damp—young stock for replacements is also a reason for the demand.

When I joined my father, in 1926, amongst the new stocks bought in to form the nucleus of the plant growing side I was bent on working up, was a Nepeta under the name of 'Souvenir d'Andre Chaudron'. I chose it from the catalogue of the French firm Barbier & Co., of Orleans, who at that time, with Turbat & Co. offered nursery stock well below English wholesale prices. This Nepeta was quite different from *mussinii,* having taller spikes, larger flowers, and roots inclined to wander. The Catmint smell was even more pungent. Maybe this acted as a sales deterrent, together with the inbred conservatism of gardeners, but whatever the reason, sales were never more than a tiny fraction of N. *mussinii.* When the time came to build up stocks once more in 1946-7, I ordered a few items from Wayside Gardens of Ohio, U.S.A., who were also customers, and amongst those received was what I believed to be another new Nepeta, named 'Blue Beauty'. But when it flowered it proved to be identical with 'Souvenir d'Andre Chaudron', and later came the admission that it was the same—the change having been made simply because the original name was in itself a drag on sales.

Some English nurserymen have made similar changes quite arbitrarily. About 1939 there came a new German Phlox with the name 'Frau Alfred von Malthner', but this very soon was dropped in favour of 'Spitfire', along with Penstemon

'Garnet' for 'Andenken en Hahn', and 'Firebird' for 'Schonholzeri'. As a nurseryman one has to sympathize, and one of the rules of nomenclature now internationally agreed upon is that cultivar names should be limited to two words. The Nepeta would then be referred to as simply 'André Chaudron', which would have been less of a mouthful, though not so sales-attractive as 'Blue Beauty', which most nurserymen have now accepted. A problem has arisen in Britain over difficult continental names for cultivars, most of which have come from Germany. I have imported several German novelties, but though never guilty of an actual change of name, have translated them into English before being catalogued, where the German was difficult to pronounce and where translation was possible. Out of consideration I should have given the original in brackets when making up a catalogue. German nurserymen are very punctilious in this respect — even to giving the raiser's name as well, where known. My lapse once gave rise to the embarrassment of having to tell a German trade customer that a certain plant under an English name which he had included in his order was in fact the same as one he already had in his catalogue, of which mine was a translation.

I have yet to meet a German or Swiss nurseryman who is not an enthusiastic plantsman as well, and apart from being very friendly folk they have an admiration for British gardens and gardeners. Several send regular orders for anything new or to be recommended as additions to what they grow. They formed an association a few years ago, called the International Stauden (Hardy Plant) Union, and invited British participation. Its objects were to undertake researches and to spread information for mutual benefit, and to have occasional tours and social gatherings. I tried to get other English nurserymen to join, but though not a very active member myself, my firm is the only one left now as a British subscriber to the I.S.U.

The Germans, Dutch and Swiss do their best to keep up with the ever-changing nomenclature at the hands of the botanists and taxonomists. I make little or no effort because I believe that botanic names are difficult enough anyway for non-professionals to use, and any further changes are detrimental. Common usage should be paramount, in my view. This is not to say I'm in favour of using common or non-botanic names, endearing as some English names are. This would lead to hopeless confusion, simply because there are not enough English names to cover the many species that exist in cultivation. for example, "monkshood" can but be a collective name for the genus *Aconitum,* of which there are dozens of species — and sub-species — most of which are virtually incapable of being Anglicized. Even if they could be the result would often be clumsier than the Latin. Latin is not always the basis, since some are of Greek origin. But no matter. The important thing is that the official nomenclature is universally accepted as the only rational system. In accepting this, there is no real need to cavil as I've done, at those who seem bent on upsetting well-established names by following what most of us feel are inconsequential rules. All gardeners are free to continue using an older, more familiar name if they so wish, and fall into line only if and when it suits us to do so.

Name changing comes harder on the nurseryman than anyone else, and the wider the range he grows, the more difficult it is for him. To compile a catalogue whilst keeping up with name changes is a real headache. In order to lessen the confusion for his customers as far as possible, he has to insert both the old and new names, with bracketed synonyms for species, and cross references for the first or generic name. He knows that this may confuse or annoy some readers, yet he may risk being called to task for being out of date by the purists. It is for these reasons that I tend to take the line of least resistance by sticking to common usage — the older, better known names — at least until I think readers are willing to accept a new name which is gradually taking over. And if acceptance fails to come — as with Meconopsis *baileyi* and Nepeta *mussinii* — then I'm quite content to stick with them regardless.

I like to think that nurserymen, in the true sense, are of a different order to some who call themselves by that name, but are not. A true nurseryman nurses plants, and rears them for sale as plants, whether they are trees, shrubs, outdoor or indoor plants, or even tomato plants, for sale as such. But if he grows the tomatoes themselves for sale, or any kind of vegetable, fruit or flower as a crop, then he is not a nurseryman: he is a market gardener or grower, because he markets produce that is cut, gathered, or picked. There is much more than a subtle difference between the two, though in some cases he may be both nurseryman and market gardener, and he cannot claim to be entirely devoted to either, since there is a clear-cut distinction between the two activities. There are, however, at least a dozen types of nurserymen, if one takes in the specialists in the many fields of horticulture, from fruit and vegetable plants to climbers, orchids, and forest and other trees. I heard of one nurseryman who grew nothing but privet hedging for sale — and pitied him. At the other end of the scale, the firm of Hilliers of Winchester stand supreme, with catalogues covering several thousands of different kinds and types of plants, trees and shrubs. Such general nurserymen are becoming extremely thin on the ground, and it would be as much, if not more of a loss to horticulture if Hilliers cut back or packed up, as if Harrods closed down as a leading retail store.

As a general rule, nurserymen cannot claim a high rating for long establishment. A rough check in my records revealed that over thirty per cent of those on my mailing list, to whom I sent catalogues previous to 1940 are no longer in business. Such a high fall-out rate is due to two reasons that come to mind. One is that a good many amateurs turn professional, even if only in a small way, and when they retire or die, the business dies with them. In other cases a family business folds up for lack of heirs willing to work hard at a not very profitable trade, and many firms with nurseries on the outskirts of towns become swallowed up in suburbia. Even if owners resisted the temptation to sell up for building land, Councils have powers of compulsory acquisition — as I discovered to my cost at Oakington. When I decided to move from there in 1946 the Council grabbed it immediately and prevented me from selling it on the open market. It was two years before they paid for it — at well

One of the nursery fields at Bressingham.

The 'modern' frame yard of nursery, 1974.

below market price. Having vacated it, the weeds took over, and the still-existing "War Ag." attempted to penalize me on this account as I was still the legal owner.

"New Zealand Flax" is one of several common names inclined to give a wrong impression. Flax comes to mind as a flowering plant, (already mentioned as Linum, in Chapter Eleven), of quite low stature, but used in this context it has no connection, except in its commercial properties. As Phormium, (a member of Liliaceae), it is a native of New Zealand, but cultivation elsewhere has been in order to extract the fibre from the leaves which is one of the strongest rope-making materials in nature. Growth of Phormium *tenax* is rather like a huge evergreen Iris, with blades two to three inches wide and up to six feet tall in my garden. These leaves are glaucous and tough in the extreme. Spikes carrying not-very-large, yellow flowers tower a foot or two even higher, strong and straight above the equally erect fanned-out foliage. It must be a fine sight on the little Island of St Helena, where it is said to be the staple crop. In Britain it is not quite reliably hardy, but is easy enough to protect through the coldest of winters, given litter around the plants six to eight inches deep.

The species *colensoi* is therabouts hardy, and though much dwarfer in every way, at about 2½ feet, it flowers more freely than P. *tenax*. Both will come from seed, but the latter is capable of variation to include bronzy-purple and striped with buff or gold. There is also a pygmy to which the name 'Baby Bronze' has been given which grows well under two feet. I find these Phormiums of great value in the garden—statuesque, permanent and trouble-free, given a reasonably good deep soil, not too heavy, nor too dry in summer. Some good variegated forms I have will with luck one day increase sufficiently to offer. But patience is needed, for a single fan may take three years to yield two divisions. They will not be hurried, and seedlings of these mostly revert to a plain, unmarked shade of colour.

Some Orchis I have grown or tried to grow will not be hurried, either. The name Orchis has been axed, by the way, in favour of Dactylorrhiza, which means "fingered root", but Orchis it remains as far as I'm concerned, for an obvious reason. These stumpy, fingered roots of such Orchis as *fuchsii,* (or *maculata*) *foliosa,* and *madierensis* produce one flower spike and then rot away, but in the process one, and perhaps two more younger crowns or roots have formed, to flower the following year.

Since coming to Bressingham these entrancingly beautiful plants with their close-set spikes of lilac to violet-purple flowers, lipped and speckled, have ranked amongst my favourites. It was a thrill to find, when I first wandered over the farm in 1946, that in a disused sunken lane, boggy and bushy in places, a quite large colony of wild Orchis was established. They varied a little in shade and height, from a foot to about twenty inches. Having no comparable garden conditions at that time, I allowed them to stay untouched for a few years. But when the Dell Garden began, I then marked a few of the finest with sticks, when in flower, in June, and dug them out in autumn to plant in semi-shade where the soil was damp. They were identified at first as Orchis *maculata,* and they flourished, increasing so quickly that the group of about thirty produced about three hundred after three years. These were planted in nursery rows in what I believed would be suitable conditions, but they sulked and gradually died away. The thirty which were reserved for replanting the group likewise failed, but this I put down to an over-liberal use of compost.

Since then, the best Orchis from this wild stock, (now reckoned to be O. *fuchsii*), have come from self-sown seedlings, which have appeared here and there where soil has not been disturbed — often in with some other plant. From a swop with Glasnevin Botanic Garden in Ireland, I obtained nine roots of the slightly earlier-flowering Orchis *elata,* which with its taller poker spikes of rich violet, out-shone any other I had seen. Every autumn I lifted half the group alternately, and so enlarged it that after a few years I had to find another place for the increase. By this means, lifting a portion every year, after twelve years, about fifty could be spared for sale, and in the four years since then a similar number over and above a fairly constant basic stock of several hundreds; there has never been more than a hundred to spare for sale. I doubt if it will ever increase beyond this figure, but at least I am able to share its precious beauty with a few enthusiasts.

The same slow, but intriguing and challenging process is under way with O. *foliosa* and O. *madierensis,* but it will be several years yet before any of these can be spared, even if luck still holds. With three other species I acquired there was total failure. These had been collected wild in the Dolomites and Appenines, but they refused to become integrated at all at Bressingham. One of these was the dwarf, purple, May-flowering Orchis, with its delightful perfume. This I'd first met as a boy, in one damp meadow on the edge of the Fens where I lived, but the meadow was later drained and ploughed, and the Orchis was never seen again round there. These hardy Orchis, by the way, should not be confused with Orchids. They belong to the same family, but are totally different from any native to warmer climates and the name Orchid applies only as a collective. This family, Orchidaceae, is a vast one of over six hundred genera with about 16,000 known species attached to them.

CHAPTER FOURTEEN

Phlox, Pyrethrum . . . .

PROBABLY more perennial plants come under P than any other letter. Alphabetically the Paeonias take precedence, and as a garden subject have many virtues. Though a long-flowering season is not one of them, by having different species there can be Paeonias in flower from April to July. Large flowers, rich and beautiful shades of colour, and in many a perfume as well, make them well loved by nearly all gardeners. Their permanence is an outstanding feature, for given an open site in reasonably strong or deep soil they can be left down for years. I have seen some, still flowering strongly, which the owner assured me had been undisturbed for over fifty years.

The most popular range have been bred from P. *lactiflora*, which was introduced from Asia in 1548. These are mostly June-flowering, double, and often scented. Named varieties are legion—some being raised well over a hundred years ago and still in cultivation. The French, as well as the Americans and British, went in for breeding, but since it takes three to five years for a seedling to germinate, grow and flower, and it can only be increased by division, it is a very slow process to build up a stock for distribution. The earliest of relatively recent introduced species is the trickily-named P. *mlokosewitschii* which was found in 1907 in the Caucasus. This charmer is a satiny light yellow, with glaucous foliage, carried on 2-2½ foot stems, and it is a thrill even to see the first shoots emerging, plump and purple-red, in February and March.

Fifty years ago some specialists listed two hundred or more named varieties. Two of the leading firms were Kelways of Langport and Artindales of Boston, but though Kelways are still flourishing and still Paeony specialists, Artindales were amongst several who offered a wide range of perennials between the wars, they and several more are now but a memory. Some of the fifty or so kinds once listed in my own firm's wholesale catalogue have also become just a memory. The fact is that nursery producers have been forced to cut back, because it is now quite uneconomic to grow a wide range of varieties even of popular groups. Whilst I am thankful that my sons back my belief that it is vitally important for us to maintain a wide collection of species, I am willing to sink the pride I used to take in offering a multitude of cultivars as well. This was when it was quite prestigious and to some extent profitable to do so, but those times have passed. In the present circumstances hand labour has to be cut to the barest minimum, but the wider the variety one grows on a nursery the greater the labour requirement. When growing a range of cultivars, whether Paeonies, Michaelmas Daisies, Iris, Phlox and the like, many are so much alike, and a careless slip or two when handling them dormant, causing a mix-up which flowering-time reveals, can cause endless trouble and loss before it is corrected. Paeonias are especially difficult to sort out, because so few divisions, planted up in the early autumn will flower the following summer. If any appear to have become mixed, they have to be left down for a further year, before they can be "rogued" or sorted out. The range of Paeonies has been cut back to about thirty named varieties, but a few more species have been added.

There was a time when I grew and listed over eighty varieties of Border Phlox. These are capable of being propagated much more quickly than Paeonies, and new varieties are continually being raised. The number of these I've stocked and listed over the years is well over two hundred, with limitations being made by dropping old and inferior ones as new or better ones come out. Now, the process of keeping a range of the most reliable growers, distinct in colour from each other, has pruned the catalogue list down to a mere twenty-eight. And if we grow up to ten thousand of each of some, the time spent on producing such quantities is much less than when there were eighty varieties to cope with. It is still pretty tedious, for each one has to be handled three or four times during the process of lifting, grading, and slicing up roots to be bedded in frames to use for planting up six months later.

Phlox do well at Bressingham, for they enjoy our light sandy soil, which does not dry out. They are not happy on heavy clays, nor do they flourish so well where chalky. And we found to our cost that they sometimes object to the Simazine types of weedkiller. It came as a hope, about 1961, that this would solve the weed problem, and first experiments were successful. But a block of about 80,000 Phlox planted in autumn 1961 was sprayed with Simazine to prevent seedling weeds. No weeds had appeared by March, but nor did the Phlox which should have been through by then. Only a fraction lived, and as we pondered the answer came. The first two weeks of March 1962 were of clear days and frosty nights. As the top-soil froze and then thawed the Simazine must have become active and lethal by penetrating more deeply than it would otherwise have done.

There are two Phlox varieties which cannot be increased from root cuttings. One is 'Nora Leigh', which we first saw at Broadwell in the Cotswolds. Joe and Joan Elliott were keen for me to take it up, since they and Mrs Leigh, who was Joan's mother, believed it worthy of an Award of Merit, as well as of wider distribution. The flowers were small, of a washy pale lilac shade, but the foliage was so brightly variegated that the colour of the plant was almost entirely primrose yellow, making the flowers of no significance. It had been a favourite for Mrs Leigh for the whole of her long life, since she'd brought it from her parents' garden in Devon.

I soon discovered, on growing it at Bressingham, that any new growth that sprang from a severed root came green-leaved, which meant it could only be increased by taking tip cuttings in spring, or dividing. There was danger in the latter method, because if a broken root happened to be left in a divided piece this

Phlox 'Nora Leigh' (in August) introduced by author.

Phlox 'Harlequin' a variety raised at Bressingham with violet purple flowers and variegated leaves.
Gardeners Chronicle

would shoot with green foliage, and become difficult to take out. But tip cuttings were slow to make up into plants, variegation being a kind of disease — chlorophyll deficiency — growth was less vigorous. 'Nora Leigh' gained the A.M.R.H.S., but what pleased its namesake did not please those who planted it on heavy or alkaline soil, even though the plants we sent out were two years old from cuttings. What grew quite well here were disappointing in some people's gardens.

Then Percy Piper discovered another one in some seedlings he'd raised, with less variegation, but a stronger habit and quite showy violet-purple flowers. This I increased, and having named it 'Harlequin' decided to offer this instead of 'Nora Leigh'. But the group of the latter in my garden still attracted, and after a lapse of four years, she had to come back for those with suitable soil who were still keen to have it. And just as a tail piece, I later spotted the identical plant in Munich Botanic Garden, labelled Phlox *paniculata* 'variegata', which according to the then curator, Wilhelm Schact, had been there for almost a century.

He is one of those unforgettable characters, and made many friends in England. I first met him in 1955, when acting as a guide for a party of visiting German nurserymen and botanists. He was easily the most knowledgeable one in the party, and with his booming voice and persuasive arguments could still any disagreement over plant identification. Before 1939 he was gardener to King Boris of Bulgaria, and after retirement took over the management of a large private garden on the Italian Lakes. One unforgettable experience he gave Flora and I was to take us by jeep up to the Schachen Alpine Garden in the Bavarian Alps, high above Garmisch.

Previous to 1939 hundreds of acres of Pyrethrums were grown as cut flowers for market, especially in Cambridgeshire. Looking back, one wonders how the markets absorbed the vast quantities of flowers sent in, during the three weeks or so when cutting took place. Usually the earliest brought the best returns, but if warm weather came there was invariably a glut, and this often coincided with Whitsun. They might well fetch twelve to fifteen shillings a box if sent before Whitsun, but afterwards, with a lapse of three or four days because of the holiday weekend, they could be down to three or four shillings — for a box of three of four dozen bunches.

When switching over from market growing to producing plants in the early 1930's there was still a demand for Pyrethrums. I set out to grow a wide variety because market growers were keen enough to try anything new or outstanding. In 1939 I had well over thirty, including doubles and singles, but although stocks were severely cut during the war, I believed the demand for plants would be greater than ever when peace returned. So it was — for a time. In the early 1950s I bought a lorry-load just for stock. They were old plants made available when a Dover nursery packed up, but they also included some old varieties. By 1953, still believing I was on the right lines, forty varieties were offered, totalling about 100,000 plants. In those days I spent all the time I possibly could with the "splitting gang" — selected helpers whose job it was in spring to divide what was left from sales into planting pieces to grow on for the following year. Pyrethrums were an important part of this seasonal task and because so much had to be done in a few crucial weeks, I used to work fourteen or fifteen hours a day, seven days a week, between February and May.

It was in 1953 that I learned of a new salmon-coloured Pyrethrum in Denmark, named 'Evenglow', (in its English translation), and took a trip over there to clinch distribution rights for the U.K. Though as a cut flower it proved disappointingly weak-stemmed, plants sold well and the outlay was recovered within a year or two. But from that time on Pyrethrums began to go into a decline from two aspects. The first was that of demand. Cut flower growers were beginning to find labour costs disproportionate to their market returns. In addition there were rumours of a sickness in stock, which lost vigour for no accountable reason. Till then, what I grew had been vigorous enough, but some suffered during a very wet winter — just as the target I'd set of 150,000 plants had been reached.

By the late 1950s a batch of seedlings we'd raised from 'Evenglow', after crossing this with some richly-coloured double varieties, were showing great promise. I named them 'Ariel', 'Prospero', 'Vanessa', 'Venus' and 'Bellarion' as soon as there were enough to offer, each worked up by division from one original plant. But just then the "sickness" came in to spoil things. At first I doubted if it was a disease, for not all were affected, and there were symptoms which could have been put down to some soil or mineral deficiency. But all the remedies I tried failed to arrest the decline, much less restore them to the healthy vigour they had previously enjoyed.

Over the past ten years Pyrethrums have for me become a sad story and a baffling experience. The fall in the demand may have been offset by the fact that we could no longer grow them successfully, but it was still hard to take. For two or three years we had none worth offering, yet I couldn't bring myself to scrap the lot and be done with them. Instead, I've hung on to the remnants of a score or so of some varieties, to a few hundred of others, always hoping some cure would be found by the pathologists to whom plants were sent. It has been baffling because odd plants and one or two varieties occasionally break into fresh vigour, and the sickness is one which seems to retard growth, rather than destroy it. Undoubtedly it is the same sickness which began to afflict the market growers twenty years ago, nearly all of whom gave up trying to grow Pyrethrums. But here and there one hears of nurserymen still able to produce healthy plants. One of these, whom I visited in 1974, near Kassel in Germany, grew them as small plants in pots. Another nursery a few miles from Bressingham was begun by two of our employees who went into partnership after learning the trade here. They have so far maintained healthy stocks, being on fresh land perhaps, but I fancy it will catch up with them too.

When seeking expert advice on plant diseases, it is mostly a case of sending specimens to be studied by pathologists. But so often the advice, when it comes, is that we should dig up and burn all infected stock. Or it may be to detach at the base all infected growth, and use some spray of dust on what remains. But nothing so far has come for Pyrethrum sickness, and just as the recommended treatment is so drastic or difficult to apply on a large scale, so hopes of combating or curing such diseases remain at a very low ebb. But there is some comfort to be had. Relatively speaking, very few hardy plants are liable to diseases. It's just that the few that are stand out like a sore thumb.

I know of no disease that affects Polygonums, but I can think of some, in this large and varied Knotweed genus, which are themselves a pest. One is the tall P. *cuspidatum,* which has become a wild menace in Cornwall, defying eradication. P. *sachaliense* is similar, and though the dwarfer and quite pretty P. *reynoutria* is still grown commercially, I have been obliged to have the group in my garden dug out, because it was so invasive. Some people may well have been duped into planting another Polygonum as a quick-cover, flowering climber. The trouble with "Russian Ivy", Polygonum *baldschuanicum* is that it never knows when to stop, and will mostly go far beyond the original purpose for which it was recommended.

When excavating an addition to my big pond in 1955 there was a patch of a wild Knotweed which never flowered. It was nothing to worry about, and I imagined that by digging down nearly three feet just there that would be the end of it. But not so. Soil was replaced by water, and when summer came again so did the Knotweed, and as the shoots reached surface, with their spear-shaped leaves floating, so came little spikes of pink flowers. This gave the clue to its identity, for I'd known there was a species named Polygonum *amphibium,* and this was it.

If many of the 150 or so species of Polygonum are either too weedy or too dull for gardens, some are first rate subjects, and a few are in the category of choice. Of the latter, two are quite outstanding, and anyone with the kind of soil and situation they like is missing out if they do not grow them. P. *milettii* like moisture, good soil and a little shade. From quite tough semi-woody clumps come narrow, deep green leaves in spring, and by late May the first red pokery spikes are showing. These reach about twelve inches in June, and from then on flowering is almost continuous until autumn. Though long-lived and hardy a large clump is often difficult to divide because the shoots are based not above the roots, as one would expect, but spring from below, making it necessary to trace them to their source before inserting a knife. It seldom sets seed, and these two factors are likely to keep it rare as well as choice.

P. *sphaerostachyum* is less fussy, and will grow in any good soil, either in sun or partial shade. Shoots appear more or less in orthodox fashion, and the clumpy habit makes division less tricky than for P. *milettii,* which is just as well, for it sets no seed at all in my experience. For flowering display it is a treasure. Beginning in May, the

The maroon coloured Trillium *sessile* and Primula *sieboldii* 'Snowflakes'.

branching stems carry an almost endless succession of little bright pink pokers, up to twenty inches or so, and bushing outwards as well. A trimming back with a little feeding if need be will bring still more stems to prolong the show until autumn frosts arrive.

A third Polygonum, also choice for good moist soil, is P. *macrophyllum*. This is not quite so free to flower, but the pokers of clear pink rise to 18 inches above narrow, deep green leaves a foot or so long, prettily waved and crinkled. It has the same clumpy habit and presents no real difficulty when large enough to divide. These three are of proven merit as far as my experience goes, but I have two or three more, quite obscure species, distinct and so far very attractive, which I hope to be able to recommend in the fullness of time, for they too are slow to increase.

It is this kind of anticipation which makes hardy perennials so fascinating for me. No doubt others feel the same way, and I cannot imagine it applying to such a degree in any other section of decorative gardening. Maybe it does, but I'm not ashamed of being biassed in favour of perennials, and glad that the Hardy Plant Society, which I helped to form in 1957, and of which I was the first Chairman, is still increasing its membership.

Amongst my many favourites are Potentillas, which include alpine, herbaceous and shrubby kinds. The latter are in great demand for their neatness and long-flowering, but though such alpine types as P. *tonguei, verna, ternata* and *nitida* are charming, it is the intermediate hybrids that have a special appeal for me. Whilst still a schoolboy, I spent ten shillings of my savings in buying one of each of twelve kinds from the then famous firm of Prichard. Most of them were hybrids, raised in Victorian times, by English, French and Belgian hybridists, which indicates a popularity then which, for some reason I fail to understand, scarcely exists now.

I still have most of those original twelve varieties — 'Mons. Rouillard', 'Flambeau', 'Wm. Rollison', 'North Star', 'Gloire de Nancy' as well as others acquired since then. All have strawberry-type leaves and short, branching stems carrying flowers in the richest shades imaginable, from pure yellow to orange flame, mahogany red to crimson scarlet. Some are double, others are single-flowered, from one to two inches across, and all flower for several weeks in summer. P. 'Gibson's Scarlet' is still popular, and at nine inches or so is dwarfer than most. It took its name from George Gibson of Leeming Bar, Yorks., but this was disputed by the nearby firm of Harkness, from which George Gibson broke away to become a rival. John Harkness once told me that a Captain Pinwillis had raised it, and it should have been known as 'Pinwillis Scarlet'. Maybe sour grapes came into it. Both firms grew a large range of plants, but neither survived their founders.

Primulas have such a wide appeal that almost any keen gardener would have a favourite or two amongst the vast range in existence. I have had no success with some that may well be other people's favourites, preferring to blame unconducive climatic conditions, rather than lack of skill on my part. But the fact that the forms of P. *sieboldii* are amongst my favourites is not only because these charmers grow well for me. My group of P. *s.* 'Snowflakes', backed by one of the maroon Trillium *sessils,* with Corydalis *cashmeriana* shining ethereal blue in front, is a gladdening sight, in the most worrisome days of the spring rush of work.

PRIMULA ROSEA
DELIGHT

CHAPTER FIFTEEN

Rose, Rheum . . . .

FOR SOME, Roses would rank as the most important subject under the letter R. For others it would be Rhododendrons. The latter have a rather aristocratic connotation. Not only do some of those who grow them think of them as aristocratic in relation to most other shrubs, but so many rhodophiles are aristocratic themselves, in standing as gardeners if not in title or heritage. Snobbery is inclined to show itself here and there, and those of us who are outside the club fail to understand the disdain some of its members appear to have for what are to them the lower orders of decorative subjects. With Rhododendrons and Azaleas in the top bracket, are often included Primulas and Lilies and a few more select plants which keep a kind of natural or satellite company with them. Being somewhat cussed by nature, I find it rather amusing, for though I fancy Rhodos would grow quite well on the neutral Bressingham soil, I have deliberately avoided them.

There is not the same aura with Roses, for they are grown and loved by all and sundry. But my reason for growing only a very few is the same. It is simply that it would have been quite out of character for me not to have given perennials and alpines pride of place, knowing also that no large garden existed where they were given precedence. There are probably more than twenty acres of Rhododendrons and Roses to be seen up and down the country to every one of hardy perennials and alpines. Nor do I grow other popular subjects such as Dahlias, Gladiolus, and Chrysanthemums, though I have one or two species of them. I also keep off all annual and so-called bedding plants.

Years ago I grew a tiny Rose named 'roulettii', which produced almost double flowers over an inch across, but never exceeded six inches high. This I lost, but have kept a few of the slightly taller Rosa *pumila,* with similar pink flowers. Back in 1933 an old lady came to the nursery, and on seeing it said she'd like one to keep company with a double red of similar habit which had been in her garden for forty years. A swop was arranged; a nice plant of Rosa *pumila* for some cuttings from her red one, which we decided should be called 'Oakington Ruby'. Len Smith, who had come as a helper even before he left school, was by now showing skill as a propagator, and from those twenty cuttings in 1933 he had produced over a thousand young plants by 1934, with another thousand or more cuttings being rooted.

I took 'Oakington Ruby' to the R.H.S. Hall, where it was given the much-coveted Award of Merit. We were elated, and intensive propagation

Pot grown alpine plants in frames, Bressingham.

continued, along with advertising to the trade, in the firm belief that it would be a much-needed money spinner. But no more than a couple of hundred were sold that year. The total stock, by early 1935, was around five thousand, and disheartened, we took no more cuttings. They were growing in three-inch pots, and in rooting through the drainage hole became unshapely and difficult to take out for sale. In fact, they became unsaleable, and then suddenly orders began to come in. By picking out the smallest a few were sent out, but when Dobbies of Edinburgh ordered five hundred we had to decline, rather than risk a complaint. There was quite a vogue for these miniature Roses just before 1939 and after 1945, and many new names appeared. But apart from three or four which have proved reliable, including 'Oakington Ruby', I'm not bothered with them, either in the garden or nursery.

It meant a great deal to me, as a young nurseryman, to gain an Award of Merit for a plant I'd raised and introduced. I imagined it as a kind of Hallmark, whether given by the appropriate Committee at the R.H.S. Hall or at Chelsea, or after trial at Wisley. The certificates for the few obtained before 1939 I proudly tacked up on the wall of my office at Oakington, but they were lost in the move to Bressingham. When in 1950 I set out wholeheartedly to restore the nursery business once more I was again keen to collect more Awards, if only as a means of publicity for new plants, and several more were gained before I began developing the new garden. Then, with an ever-increasing range of new kinds arriving, including uncommon species, I submitted any I considered worthy of such recognition, though I can fairly say that I did not do so for personal gain. But, as many more Award Certificates were received I slowly realized that they made very little difference to sales.

However, this was not the main reason why, after a year or two, I stopped sending up flowers or plants of uncommon subjects. A well-known professional gardener paid me a first-time visit. He was also interested in hardy perennials, and for a time I enjoyed showing him around. I knew that he, too, had submitted a good many plants for Award, but not, I discovered that day, for a wholly worthy reason. He let the cat out of the bag by asking unashamedly if I would let him have any good and out of the ordinary kinds so that he could add to the score of Awards he'd already gained.

"The record", he said, "stands at eighty-three. I want to beat that — and maybe make it up to a century."

I'm not much of an altruist, but this jarred. Any R.H.S. Award for a subject already in cultivation is, or should be, for the plant itself, and not for the person who enters it. But because that person's name is on the Certificate and on any press report, the temptation is to make capital out of it. Of course it's different in cases where new plants are bred and introduced. The raiser is then fairly entitled to recognition, as well as the subject he has bred and introduced. But to collect Awards for record-breaking purposes seemed wrong to me, and apart from not giving in to this request, I've never submitted any more plants since then on chance of gaining an Award. Some more Certificates have come, but only when the R.H.S. has held invited Trials of various genera, but I've no idea how many there are tucked away, unprized, in a drawer in the office. Some First Class Certificates lie there too, and these rank even higher than Award of Merit.

What matters most is garden merit, but this is something on which it is scarcely safe to generalize. The Council of the R.H.S. must have been thinking on these lines when making a list of subjects worthy of the Award of Garden Merit. Unlike the plain A.M., which has also been given to subjects which for one reason or another never became distributed or made available to gardeners, the A.G.M. is for those which have stood the test of time and varying garden and climatic conditions. It applies to more or less the whole range of hardy plants, trees and shrubs, and after a lapse of some years its Special Committee was reformed. I was amongst the twenty or thirty members asked to serve, but though meetings were quite infrequent, after the first one, attendance began to dwindle. Every subject on the list which each session had before it, was voted upon after any discussion it might raise.

In theory it was a good idea that Committee members voted one way or the other only if they'd had practical experience of the subject in question. But in practice, as attendance at meetings tailed off, it did not work out very well, because judgement of less well known subjects fell to perhaps only three or four members who had grown it. So it is that some to which the A.G.M. has been awarded, as a guide to the less knowledgeable gardeners on the look out for good, reliable subjects, have gained it by one vote, regardless of how many votes were cast. But there, one must accept that, whatever Award may or may not be given to hardy garden plants of any type, the final test lies with the individual who tries it in his or her own garden. The R.H.S. does its best to assist and advise, but it is composed, from Council to Sub-Committee and staff, of experts in their own field. There is no such thing as an all-round expert, for the range is far too wide for anyone to possess more than a portion of knowledge, even as a specialist in a particular section. The more one learns about plants, the greater this awareness of how much still lies beyond one's knowledge grows. It is the awareness, coupled with the joys of cultivating, that keeps the mind alert, receptive, and constantly stimulated.

Successes with the rare or less easy plants are sweet, but if failures are sad to behold, sometimes even these can act as a stimulant. So often it has to be a case of trial and error, and I made more than one successive error before I finally succeeded with Ranunculus *aconitifolius* 'plenus' — also known as 'Fair Maid of France', (sometimes 'of Kent'). Although belonging to the same genus as the yellow Buttercup, this one has flowers of purest white — and of the most perfect double formation imaginable. It has deeply-incised leaves, and in May stems rise to branch quite widely, carrying such an abundance of flowers, barely ½-inch across, that the whole becomes a snowy mound in May and June. It was not happy in the wet, rather sticky soil where I first planted it. I tried it next time in a lighter soil with plenty of compost and an open position, but it resented this too, sending weakly stems to only twelve inches. But when I mixed in both peat and leaf mould, with moisture not far below, up it came to full glory, over two feet tall and as far across when in flower.

Rodgersias are relatively easy, given some shade, a rich soil, and moisture, They expand steadily, with hard fleshy crowns only just below surface, and send up long stalks topped with broad fingery leaves — rather like those of the Chestnut tree. Leaves alone will come up to nearly three feet, and a foot or two above these, in June and July, come plumes of creamy white or pink in a few clones of R. *pinnata*, such as R. *p.* 'superba'. This and 'Irish Bronze' have leaves more colourful, and the flowers are decidedly aromatic, especially in R. *pinnata* 'elegans'. To keep Rodgersias happy and handsome all they need is a mulching in early spring.

By contrast, the Roscoeas die back to clustered, fleshy roots sitting six inches or more below surface. They are amongst the latest perennials to reappear in spring, but when they do, growth of the sheathed leaves is rapid enough. Through these come some exotic-looking flowers on stiff stems, having a prominent lip, and remaining colourful for several weeks. Not that any of the species are brilliant, for R. *cautleoides,* the earliest, is lemon-yellow, and R. *procera,* (or *purpurea*), is soft violet-purple. R. *beesiana* is both primrose and purple, and the soft mauve R. *humeana,* of leek formation, are also under two feet. They are not fussy plants, and seem happy in either sun or partial shade, but though the nine-inch R. *alpina,* with pinkish flowers, can be rather a nuisance for not keeping itself to itself, the others raise no problems. As a genus it has curiosity as well as decorative value. It is said to be the only hardy member of the Ginger family, apart from its cousin, the Cautleya. The fangy roots are very brittle, and if one is snapped, it immediately exudes a yellowish sap, which looks as if it should be good for some purpose, though so far as I know it has no properties of value, medicinal or otherwise.

Ruscus is the simple Latin name for "Butcher's Broom", which has now become quite scarce. It will put up with quite arid conditions beneath trees and still remains evergreen, slowly expanding into a huge clump. Perhaps it has become scarce because it grows so slowly and because it is adaptable to the most difficult positions. Its small but prickly leaves and pencil-thick stems will rise to about three feet, and although these will carry red, holly-sized berries, I've never seen any on mine. On R. (or Danea) *racemosa*, (Alexandrian Laurel), the leaves are not prickly, and are larger and shiny. The stems are less stiffly erect, and as an evergreen, half way to being a shrub, it is quite delightful, and much sought after by florists for Christmas decorations. I first grew it at Oakington, but only a dozen or so plants remained in 1946 to bring to Bressingham.

Having hand-dug a foul piece of ground behind the garage, on the south of some horse chestnut trees, I planted these remnants hopefully. They flourished, although the plant was said to be a little tender and have a preference for shade. This too, is slow to expand, but I divided the largest each year, till the whole patch was filled, totalling three or four hundred plants. After that, a few were sold to the trade, but then, in 1961, I began to collect traction engines. By the autumn there were eight hulks in need of restoration standing in the nearby farmyard. They also needed a space where they could stand side-by-side. In the belief that Danea *racemosa* would prove a profitable nursery subject, grown on a larger scale, all were dug up, divided and planted elsewhere, and thereafter steam engines took their place. But in spite of trying it in different soils and situations it has never flourished so well elsewhere. It increases sufficiently well for us to sell a number each year, but makes little greenery and remains a puzzle unsolved because some, placed in what I was advised was an ideal site, in the shade of high trees, are no better than the main stock in the open nursery.

Rheum is a genus I grow in four species. One of these, (R. *alexandrae*), is baffling, because it is so shy in flower. But when it does flower, even sparsely, it is very spectacular indeed, with its little tongues of light, creamy yellow hanging down much of the three-foot stem in May and June. It is a most attractive freak, but until it was shown at Chelsea, we seldom sold more than a dozen a year. That was when I was strictly wholesale only, and our trade customers were not interested. It was in order to make some of the uncommon plants I had, more readily available to keen amateurs that I decided to open the door a little for retail business, and after more than thirty years, put up an exhibit at Chelsea which included a plant of Rheum *alexandrae* with three flower spikes. At the time, there were about three hundred Rheum *alexandrae* in a nursery bed. On the first day all three hundred were booked as orders—and about half were for trade cutomers who, if they'd seen it listed in the catalogue, had not known how attractive it was. Two other Rheums are ornamental in a different way. The first leaves are brightly coloured, mainly red and as they become large with jagged edges, a huge spike shoots up to six or seven feet to open into a clustered plume of pink flowers. This is R *palmatum* 'rubrum', and is more colouful but less tall than the even larger R. *tanguticum*, but the leaf spread is so wide that when these become tatty and fading by July their value is somewhat cancelled out.

The fourth Rheum is the one I would never willingly part with, and though the young growth is decorative, it is not grown in the decorative part of the garden. In plain words, it is Rhubarb, and if it were possible, I would eat it as a breakfast fruit every day of the year, except at Strawberry time. It is not only because I believe it to be good to eat, but because I like it, and though my father held it in equally high esteem, I am now the only member of my family with this addiction. The variety I grow has no name, and I've had it for so long that I've forgotten where it came from. But it is early, and is planted in some good light soil at the bottom of the kitchen garden, close to the piggeries. The first picking is usually in February — or just after the few clumps placed each year in time to pick for Christmas, have finished producing, under the greenhouse stage. Outdoors, the permanent bed keeps me supplied until October, and now I'm hoping a deep freeze will fill in the gap.

Rheum   *palmatum*   'rubrum' — ornamental rhubarb.

CHAPTER SIXTEEN

Sempervivum, Sedum . . . .

FROM about Michaelmas to Easter we have the garden more or less to ourselves on Sundays. Depending on the weather, I spend most Sundays during that period following my fancy as far as work is concerned. I like digging and making bonfires when it's cold, but dry. If wet and windy, there are usually plants to be divided for the few acres of nursery I look after close to my house. This is mainly for special kinds which do not take kindly to the more open main nursery, not to mechanized planting. Sometimes I've worked up a stock till there were too many to handle, only to have it returned a year or two later, decimated or worse through having failed in the main nursery.

In autumn and spring, on most Sundays as well as weekdays, there are jobs for me in the decorative part of the garden, with its forty seven beds. It is routine now to go round bed by bed in July and August, noting down what needs to be done when summer is over, and what improvements could be made in grouping. Some groups may need rejuvenating—digging up, dividing and replanting. Others may need a move for the sake of fitness with regard to height, colour, or some other suitability factor, and losses made good. I have learned to be cautious about changing group positions. So often I've taken out a group for some good reason, only to find it starts off a chain reaction, resulting in several groups having to be moved before the first one is in just the right position in relation to its neighbours for the three essentials of height, colour and time of flowering.

On Sundays between Easter and Michaelmas I seldom enter the garden, unless it is for a quiet stroll after supper—if I'm not too weary. Although the gates are not open till afternoon, Sunday mornings are taken up by preparing engines to be steamed and other matters in readiness for the influx of several thousand visitors. Driving an engine, with up to a hundred of these people in trucks behind, round the two-mile nursery circuit every fifteen minutes is quite tiring, but to me this is infinitely preferable to being in the garden during those five open hours. It's not only that I enjoy being engine driver twice a week for a change. Some visitors chat whilst at the station. They have been known to take me for an employee, or an ex-British Railway driver, and I was once invited to join A.S.L.E.F. But a few recognize me in my boiler suit, with a grimy face beneath my driver's greasetop cap, and ask for an autograph or the answer to some gardening problem. Such questions as "What's the name of that tall blue flower at the far end of the garden?—I couldn't see the label" can be rather disconcerting. Especially if I'm watching the rise of water in the boiler, or oiling round, or filling the bunker with coal.

Author driving train for a special party of nursery visitors in 1973.   *Michael Warren*

Coal produces soot and ashes as well as steam and smoke. Time was when one could buy soot by the ton for horticultural use — and I can just remember when gasworks coke and boiler ash could be had free for the carting. Soot and ashes are no longer readily available, but there are two by-products from steam engines which are useful for the garden. Soot has high value as a soil sweetener, and vegetables — especially brassicas — respond to it almost miraculously. Ashes — the sharp, clinkery kind — are good for lightening heavy soil, for keeping slugs and snails away, and for propagating or potting soil mixes. They, and soot, need to be weathered before using with soil, but a soaking or two will also take out any toxic elements.

At Wisley they grow Sempervivums (Houseleeks) in what appears to be mainly furnace ash, and there are other alpines needing perfect drainage which will thrive in an ashy mixture. Which reminds me of a trick Will Ingwersen played, in his younger days, on his father, Walter. The latter was a recognized authority on Sempervivums and had a vast collection growing in the "hungry" mixture they like, which produces the natural size and colour of the rosettes. There was a very close relationship between father and son, but Will privily re-potted some of Walter's "Semps" into a richer mixture and then some time later asked him to name them. They were then so different in appearance that for once "Pop" Ingwersen was completely baffled.

My father used to apply soot to Sweet Peas he grew for market. He would sow seeds outdoors in autumn—mostly the then popular 'Mascott's White', in two or three rows a hundred yards or more long, and about five feet apart. Soot was applied during winter, followed by the tedious business of sticking in spring. It was the cutting and bunching that I disliked most. It was difficult to cut the full length of the stalk, and to arrange them so that the flowers all faced one way and did not overlap. Father always packed them in boxes for market himself, and though a full box was a picture, each row of bunches had to be secured with a willow stick to keep them so. Of all the flowers he grew for market Sweet Peas, despite their perfume, were those I liked least—because they were so tedious to bunch. For the same reason I disliked Raspberries and Currants amongst the various fruits he also grew. I much preferred to get stuck into a bed of annual Gypsophila, which could be pulled up by the roots to make a bunch in very little time, and I quite enjoyed

Pot grown alpine plants in the nursery at Bressingham.

chopping off the roots on the packing bench. Most of all I preferred cutting 'Stinker'. This was the double white button-flowered 'Feverfew'—Pyrethrum *parthenium*. Basal cuttings taken in autumn were planted out in spring and when ready for cutting in June all one had to do was to slash a plant off just above ground and you had a ready-made bunch. The record in one day was seventy-six large boxes of 'Stinker', on 27th June, 1927. I remember the date because I began cutting at 5.00 a.m. so as to watch a near total eclipse of the sun, and though it became almost too dark to continue cutting, I saw no eclipse because of clouds.

Schizostylis—the Kaffir Lily—is still grown for cutting. This relative of the Gladiolus and Montbretia flowers in late autumn, but the creeping rhizomes are susceptible to frost damage in severe winters. If covered with litter by the end of November in cold districts they will come through unharmed, but when in the rich, fairly moist soil they like, growth soon becomes congested, and replanting is advisable at least every other spring. But the flowers, on wiry stalks above rushy leaves are a joy—even on the original species of S. *coccinea*. This became superceded by the pink 'Mrs Heggarty', but even these are eclipsed by newer, finer ones. I came across S. 'Major' and was so impressed that it had to go up to the R.H.S. — before I gave up this practice. It gained an Award of Merit for its two-root stems and fine red flowers, and then in the nursery I spotted a clear pink one, equally tall and large-flowered. This I named 'November Cheer', for this is how it appealed to me.

The name 'Autumn Joy' has a similar connotation, and though it was first given to a hybrid Sedum as 'Herbstfreude', it means the same thing. If ever a plant was well named it is this, and it was my privilege to be able to introduce it to Britain. It was also my privilege to know the raiser, Georg Arends of Wupperthal Ronsdorf, who in my opinion was amongst the most distinguished of German plantsmen—scarcely less so than Karl Foerster. On his nursery, eight hundred feet up above the Ruhr conurbation, over thirty bombs fell during the war, smashing glasshouses and making deep craters. Yet when I first visited him in 1952 there was no bitterness against Britain, and his welcome was quite touching. He showed a little bed of a new Hydrangea, of which he'd rescued a few pieces after a bomb had destroyed a much larger stock, and asked me to introduce this as well as soon as he had sufficient. His attitude was not to bemoan a loss, but to be thankful that Hydrangea 'Preziosa' was not totally destroyed. And it pleased him greatly when in due course it received both the Award of Merit and a First Class Certificate. Every plant he raised and named was either a distinctive variation or an improvement.

Sedum 'Autumn Joy', (also A.M. and F.C.C.), has succulent grey-green growth, and in September the two-foot stems open into flattish heads a foot and sometimes more across. As the tiny flowers open they are greenish-pink and then change to a glowing salmon shade, attracting both bees and butterflies, till they fade by degrees to bronze and russet. Another Arends Sedum is the dwarfer, earlier

Sedum 'Autumn Joy', introduced to the U.K. by the author.

'Ruby Glow'; though he stuck to his original name of S. *cauticolum* 'Robustum', he agreed to my request to use 'Ruby Glow' for Britain. It was in fact a cross between the semi-prostrate alpine species cauticolum and 'Autumn Joy', and makes a splash of colour in July and August at about eight inches.

Another change was made with his Sedum *album* 'Superbum'. It was so strikingly evergreen and so valuable as a carpeter that I thought it deserved to be renamed 'Greenmantle' for English gardens.

The Sedums are nowhere near so variable as Saxifragas in character, appearance and requirements. About three hundred species of each exist, but Saxifragas differ so much that they have to be placed in sections. The Kaschia and Engleria sections are those needing sun and very gritty soil which does not dry out, even if good drainage is essential. They comprise a maze of species and cultivars, from minute silvery films or tufts to green cushions. The earliest Kaschias—white, pink and yellow—come in February, but the Englerias are a little later—and none too easy to grow. These are amongst the alpine aristocrats and are favourites for growing in pans in an alpine glasshouse.

Encrusted Saxifragas have mostly more pronounced rosettes, some very silvery, and six inches or so across in the largest. This is S. *longifolia,* which likes a crevice.

When at flowering size it sends out a shower of tiny white flowers and then alas, dies, though some hybrids are not monocarpic. Then there is the Mossy section — green-leaved and easy to grow where not parched, preferring some shade. They lack class, from the alpine enthusiasts standpoint, as one would expect, being easy to grow. The easiest of all Saxifragas is 'London Pride', S. *umbrosa,* of which there are some variations. But to my mind 'London Pride' is a very good subject, not to be despised as it sometimes is, for it will grow in dank spots where few other subjects will flourish, let alone make a display.

Amongst the non-alpine Saxifragas, S. *fortunei* and its forms appeal most to me. They make leafy mound from April to October, hiding the ground beneath. 'Wada's Variety' has a rich purple-green foliage — reddish beneath, and *rubrifolia* a coppery-red shade. They are worth growing for foliage alone, but in October they suddenly erupt, throwing up a twelve-inch spray of white flowers. Even the green-leaved type is attractive with its dual display. These are amongst the few deciduous Sxifragas, and just in case frost grips the soil deeply, they should be covered with leaves or litter during the worst winter months. In spring they will respond to some sandy peat as a mulch, for they root and feed very near the surface.

Selinum *tenuifolium* was given a First Class Certificate as long ago as 1888, yet it is rarely seen in gardens. Its common name is "Himalayan Parsley", and not very apt at that. From a fairly tough-rooted, long-lived plant, strong stems emerge in spring, which have lateral fans of the most delicate filigree leaves of deep green. At about four feet the wide, flat, whitish heads open out to stand quietly beautiful for several weeks. It has very little by way of colour, but it has much in grace and charm, and I do not think the Victorians who gave it an F.C.C. erred in their judgement.

The Victorians — gardeners included — had their faults, but their good points are at last becoming appreciated. It was an era that produced some great characters and some of these were great gardeners too. Such as William Robinson, Gertrude Jekyll, Dean Hole, Ellen Willmott and others gained fame in their own lifetime, but many, like my father, did not, though they were passionately attached to the soil as gardeners. Herbert Smith was another. He was born in 1872 — a few months after my father — and was one of the eighty with the name Smith on the register of Oakington. His nickname was "Sailor", because of his service in the Navy till about 1902. As a small holder he had the reputation of a glutton for work and a grower of quality produce, but out of the blue, in 1926, he came asking for a job. Father did not hesitate, for "Sailor" offered to come for five days a week for a mere 28 shillings — just because he longed to work amongst flowers.

By the time I had the nursery on my own in 1931 he had become almost a second father to me, and a key man as far as outdoor work was concerned. Though something of a martinet, he knew how to train others and I too learned from his store of knowledge of growth and cultivation. No work was too hard, no task too menial or tricky for him, and there were no tools he could not use expertly. Any roughness of his tongue was easily cancelled out by inner warm-heartedness and total honesty. Having reached seventy, he sold his small-holding and built a bungalow with a large garden to which he could retire, and whenever I visited Oakington after moving to Fordham the trip was incomplete without a chat with "Sailor" who still kept an eye on the nursery. My move to Bressingham caused him to say many a time how much he wished he could have come too, but we kept contact, and he slackened off work but slowly.

"I'll keep a'doin'," he'd say, when on a visit we looked round his garden, "I'll keep a'doin' as long as the Lord lets me". And it was not until he was ninety-six that the Lord decided "Sailor" had had enough.

Len Smith was the other of my stalwarts at Oakington—with the nickname of "Lightning". He was no relation to "Sailor" and became interested in plants as the son of one of my father's summer flower-pickers. When I began working up stocks of alpines in 1926 he became part-time helper, but full time as soon as he left school. He not only learned quickly, but everything he did was at "Lightning" speed. He stayed on to wind up the Oakington nursery and then joined me at Bressingham in 1947, but not for long, for his wife could not settle. But over the following years some contact was made, and then, in 1974, came the shock news of his sudden death. I'd imagined he might well outlive me, and had not until then fully realized and appreciated or acknowledged the contribution he had made. This was the obituary I felt impelled to write for the horticultural press.

OBITUARY — MR LEN SMITH

With the death of LEN SMITH the nursery trade has lost one of its most outstanding craftsmen. He was one of those rare enthusiasts who, although his skill was always applied to the firms by whom he was employed could do no other than put heart and soul into his job, as if the plants he handled were his own. My memory of him goes back to 1926, when as a twelve to thirteen year old boy whose mother worked for my parents at Oakington, he joined me in my efforts to build up stocks of Alpines and Perennials, as a section of my father's market nursery. In those early days, he plunged what I potted and inserted cuttings I prepared, and even had pumped for the watering. Before long his skill and speed in handling plants found wider expression. As a full time worker, mainly on propagating during the '30's he became "Lightning Smith" to the staff of the expanding nursery at Oakington, with foreman status on reaching his mid-twenties. Every subject he handled came as a challenge.

During the war years, with myself largely otherwise engaged Len managed the nursery, by now covering 36 acres and if stocks had to be cut to 15 per cent he not only kept this nucleus intact, but produced the vital food crops demanded with no less skill and enthusiasm, inspiring and setting the pace for others. Len Smith was outgoing and generous by nature and many have profited by his capacity for friendship and his readiness to share his knowledge. It was my pleasure to show him round at Bressingham a few short weeks ago, and to talk over old times. For old times sake, he brought me three plants of Rosa 'Oakington Ruby' knowing I had lost mine. But the news of his sudden death at little over sixty was saddening not only because of my long association with him but because men of his calibre are all too rare and the contribution they make to the success of firms fortunate enough to have the benefit of their services is seldom fully appreciated. There were times, years ago, when I took Len for granted — perhaps too much. But looking back I can see that the contribution he made in those early days was greater than I suspected. If he had lived as all who knew him would have wished, to a ripe old age, his reputation would likewise have widened. It is perhaps appropriate that I should put this tribute on record, to a man who will be sadly missed, not as a nationally known master nurseryman but as one who has played a vital part in several firms becoming nationally known.

*   *   *

There was a third person surnamed Smith who filled an important role during my time at Oakington. Ethel Smith was a Londoner and had held a good position in the office of a city firm which folded in 1934. At about forty years old she became my first book-keeper and typist, for until then these responsibilities had of necessity been mine. It took her time to readjust, but once this period passed with her increasing knowledge and interest her position became a key one in the quickly growing wholesale business. When more work came her way she took it as a compliment, and regarded long hours of work as part of the job, refusing overtime pay. She and her elder sister were friends in need when trouble came and filled many a breach for my young family. Ethel Smith too was totally honest, and my trust in her loyalty and discretion was never let down. However, when I moved to Bressingham, I had to deny these sisters their wish to come too. As spinsters their mothering instincts had, through no fault of theirs, become thwarted, and as my domestic status had become upset and complicated, I feared more trouble would follow if, in coming to Bressingham, they hoped to increase their influence. For this refusal I was never forgiven. Belatedly I tried to make my peace, but by then they had moved to Cornwall, and letters from me were not well received. Briefly polite but coldly distant replies came back, and I realized just how deeply I'd wounded them.

CHAPTER SEVENTEEN

Trillium, Trollius . . . .

AMONGST the many subjects which came as swops in 1958, when the new garden was rapidly extending, were two on which a good deal of time has since been spent, with very differing results. The visit to Ireland which Flora and I made in that year was very rewarding. In Eire, there was Glasnevin Botanic Garden and David Shackleton to visit, and in Ulster, Rowallane and Donard Nursery were outstanding. At Donard Nursery Leslie Slinger, seeing my eye settle on Thuya *orientalis* 'nana aurea', dug up three young ones for us to take back. The neat conical habit and golden hue of this little conifer appealed to me, though I was mainly on the look out for perennials. For four years they grew in a group at Bressingham with good effect, and then Adrian, my younger son, suggested that two would be best taken out, and could he have them?

He had not long since returned from his wanderings abroad, having decided after all to become a nurseryman, but also made up his mind to specialize in Conifers and Heathers. Upon reflection, I took this as a sign that he was ambitious, but did not feel inclined just to follow in my footsteps. He wanted to build up something for himself — much as I had, in joining my father. Those two Thuyas he took away, and I never saw them again — but since then, in various stages of growth from cuttings to specimens, it could be seen in several places. Of course he has worked up stocks of other conifers as well as heathers, but from those two he commandeered, he must have since produced over 100,000.

At the time he began specializing, my advice was to stick to a dozen of each of the best dwarf conifers and heathers, but though he limits the kinds he produces for sale, these are drawn from a collection now running into hundreds of different kinds — not just one dozen — but several. In one sense he has followed in my footsteps. This, however, is restricted to a matter of policy, for he believes as I do that it is only by growing a wide variety that one can prove which of them are fully garden worthy, and thus worthy to be grown in quantity for sale.

Not long after those three Thuyas were planted, there arrived a parcel from a botanic garden in Canada. It came as a result of a visit here by its Curator, who had offered to send some Trilliums in return for a few items from me. Until the new garden was made I had neither the conditions nor the time for growing such woodland plants as Trilliums, but they were amongst the subjects which for years I'd longed to grow. But what made this parcel so exciting was that it contained the rarest and choicest of them all — the double white 'Wake Robin', Trillium

The very rare Double White Trillium *grandiflorum*.

grandiflorum 'plenum'. When they flowered the following spring, I was even more convinced that this was something to treasure. The pure white flowers, 2 inches across on ten inch stems, with both petals and leaves in threes were entrancingly lovely, and stayed so for a surprisingly long time—unlike that other North American, the double white "Bloodroot" (Sanguinaria *canadensis*), which was relatively fleeting.

Naturally I could not resist digging up one or two of the largest when they became dormant again. The fleshy crowns became fatter, but there was nothing to suggest a means of increase, except to wait until new growth from the base produced rooted off-shoots. It was not until two years later that the first divisions were possible, and even these took another year or two to make up into flowering size. No wonder it had such a reputation for scarcity, I thought, but was all the more thankful that the parcel had contained fifty crowns. By about 1964 I had 150, and then lost nearly half through an unsuspected attack by slugs during their dormant period.

By 1970—after twelve years of handling them myself, increasing wherever increase by division was possible—I had close on five hundred. It was still a long way short of the target I'd set of having a basic stock of one thousand, so as to be able to sell any above this number. One had to plant different sizes in different beds, so that the small ones could remain undisturbed for two or three years, and only the third-year bed was dug up for dividing. But it was still all too slow. At this rate I might never live to be able to distribute to those who, like myself, had longed to grow it, and it was in keeping with fair distribution that a high target should be set.

So it was that in 1970 I decided to experiment. I should have tried before, but had been too timid, not daring to risk killing a flowering-sized crown by gouging out its centre, as a means of inducing new side shoots to form. I knew this method was practised with Hyacinths, but to my mind these Trilliums were far more precious. Using infinite care, I knifed about twenty, taking out the centre to prevent flowering. Some I cut into quarters, and some I left whole. In a specially sharp mixture, at the foot of a north-facing wall, I bedded them in, scattering ashes on top to keep off slugs and snails. There was no sign of growth when spring came, but a poking finger revealed they were still alive, and when this was repeated in autumn I saw some had made some tiny white shoots from below my knife cut.

The experiment had come off, but it was still relatively slow, because from the gouging operation to when the resultant new shoots, three to eight per crown, had themselves become of flowering or sale size, five years had passed. But because I was satisfied that the method was safe, and future stocks were reasonably assured, I enhanced our Chelsea exhibit of 1974 with some to sell at last. One would expect such a rarity to be difficult to grow, but this is not the case. Given some shade, not too infested with tree roots, it seems to be quite adaptable to light or heavy soil, which is not deficient in humus.

The marbled leaves of Trillium *sessile* are quite large and when the maroon, three-petalled flowers open, pointing upwards, they are a fine sight. Plants grow into quite hefty clumps twenty inches tall in my garden, and make a fine background to a group of Primula *sieboldii* 'Snowflakes', which is itself a backcloth to the marvellous blue of Corydalis *cashmeriana,* only three inches tall. All flower at about the same time — April to May.

Not far away, in humus-rich soil, never allowed to dry out, are three dwarf Thalictrum. The easiest to grow is the tiny T. *kiusianum,* carrying little flower puffs of lilac-blue on stems only an inch or two high. It creeps gently just below the surface, rooting as it goes, and the rounded, purple-green leaves become dense in time. Flowers keep coming for many weeks of summer, but T. *orientale,* though beautiful with its mauve-blue flowers and blue-green leaves, is less continuous. This too is rare, and the one plant I had several years ago has made very little spread from its fragile, tenuous root system, and has produced no seed.

T. *diffusiflorum* will set seed, but never makes much of a plant. Yet from a wispy cluster of roots, coming from a crown little larger than the size of a match head, will throw a branching spray of lavender flowers, 15-18 inches tall and twelve inches across. It is a charming plant, flowering for many weeks from June to August, and though hardy enough is not easy to please. Humus and moisture appear to be essentials for these choice little plants, and if I had no suitable place I would make a peat bed for them, and other subjects needing similar treatment.

It is in the shade and moisture range of plants that most failures have occurred with me. Maybe the East Anglian climate has been partly responsible. Many originate from valleys amongst high mountains, and whereas most of them will succeed in Scotland with a higher humidity during the growing season, the East Anglian air is very different. Winters here are often humid, or if not the east winds off the North Sea certainly do not favour any plants inclined to damp off or freeze for lack of snow cover, which we seldom have. It is this that enables some subjects to survive in such cold places as Moscow and Montreal which are not at all reliable in Eastern England.

Trollius are moisture-lovers which are amongst my favourites of those that grow well. They will in fact grow well anywhere so long as the soil is fairly rich and will survive droughty periods if mulched with peat. Their roots are not merely fibrous, for they resemble a tress of brown hair when shaken free of soil, merging into the congested crowns which produce the dome of greenery and the lovely globular buttercup flowers above. In spring they are a joy to watch as they emerge and develop, with a greenish tinge as buds, till in early May the first of them open. Altogether about thirty named varieties have been introduced and yet the range of colour is not very great. All are yellow, but vary from the orange of such as 'Fireglobe' to the pure yellow of 'Goldquelle' and the lighter 'Canary Bird'. The palest is the new 'Alabaster' also raised by Georg Arends, and though not so strong a grower as most, it has a charm of its own which few gardeners can resist. Trollius will mostly yield a second crop, by the way, if cut back when first flowering has finished. Some feed — preferably in with a light mulch and a soaking or two — will soon induce renewed flowering vigour.

Trees were a major attraction when deciding to come to Bressingham. At

Trollius — one of the author's favourite flowers.

Oakington they were sparse, and even more so in Burwell Fen, where little but thorn and sallows grew—and I rooted them out to clear more land for cropping. Fordham was less bare and the house was thereabouts girded with trees, and in leaving there, I was loath to settle in an open landscape. The oaks at Bressingham held a special appeal, for there had been none within sight of my previous homes. But apart from some fine oaks, there were pines, birch, beech, ash, sycamore, limes, alder, poplar and willow and holly. Yet within a year I was planting other kinds as well, especially conifers in variety to make for winter colour and to break the wind, for only the valley itself was wooded, and the uplands above its gently sloping side were pretty bleak. The trees nearest my house included three magnificent Huntingdon elms reaching up to a shapely hundred feet. Not far away was a row of common elm, which I quickly had felled in 1946 because they were diseased and in their place beeches were planted.

In tending the new garden I learned something more about the effect of tree roots on other plants, for in order to make use of the shade trees provided, some beds were well within their reach. Some very tall thorn and holly were in the dip known as the Dell, with oak, ash, maple and elm to draw them up. But I very soon found that cutting back tree roots where a new bed was dug out was only a temporary check. Once dug, planted and watered, tree roots quickly took advantage of it. They even beat a barrier of asbestos sheeting I let in two feet deep on the edge of one shady bed, and both ash and elm proved capable of making eight or nine feet length of new roots in one season.

Some trees are more voracious than others. In my experience ash is the most gluttonous—and the least useful tree as a shade provider. It is the last to come into leaf, and one of the first to fall. Its feeding roots are fibrous, but unlike elm and birch are easy to dig out. Trees that grow rapidly appear in general to have also the fastest-ranging roots—with birch, willow and poplar as good examples. Once these become large—along with beech and elm—curbing becomes a problem and so the selection of plants which will grow beneath them becomes much reduced.

I have one bed—in the shade of a large oak and ash tree—in which, to deprive the soil even more, is an ancient thorn tree, thirty feet tall, with a self-sown holly as company. At any time of the year the soil is dry not far below the surface and even after the wet winter of 1974-5 dust fell from the roots of some plants I lifted with a fork. But there are, nevertheless, some occupants which have to be curbed of their excessive growth and whilst others show no signs of flagging it is not to say that certain kinds I've tried there have all survived. Those that flourish are Lamiums *maculatum* and *galeobdolon*; Symphytum *caucasicum*, which is quite showy with its little pendant blue bells, on 2½ foot stems; Luzula *sylvatica* 'marginata'; and the curious "Pickaback Plant"—Tolmiea *menziesii*. This makes a massed mound of soft leaves, which after the insignificant greenish flower sprays have finished produce baby plants at the base of each leaf. Its relation, Mitella *breweri* makes neater evergreen clumps, and both Pachysandra *terminalis* and Asarum *europaeum* give good ground cover, along with Vincas and Waldsteinia *ternata.* The latter creeps, with year-round greenery, and makes a splash of yellow strawberry flowers in spring. Viola *pedata,* also yellow, and the white *pedunculata* both flower well there along with that very adaptable Campanula, *muralis,* and Trillium *grandiflorum.*

The plants from which dust fell in a wet season were a fern — Blechnum *cymosum* which has evergreen, deeply-fingered fronds up to nearly three feet. I'd been told it was rare, but was amazed to find so great a spread had occurred in so dry a place, having dug up almost a barrowful from less than half the group. The charming little 'Maidenhair Fern', Adiantum *venustum* is also happy there, creeping over and in the low flint wall I built in 1958 to hold up the bank.

Although I have forty or more of other ferns, their nomenclature is in such a muddle that it's enough to deter anyone from building up a collection. Time was, forty years ago, when Amos Perry of Enfield possessed over 2,000 species and clones, but though interest in them is growing again, only one nursery I know has a relatively small collection. I am gradually adding to my range, but would still say that four of the best are the outspreading, bright green Polystchium *setiferum* and the 'Shield Fern' and its variants, the crinkly-leaved 'Hartstongue', Phyllitis *scolopendrium* 'undulatum', the hardiest of the Maidenhair Ferns, Adiantum *pedatum,* and the hadsom 'Ostrich Plume' known as Matteuca *struthiopteris.*

Since coming to Bressingham we have never burnt anything but wood in our open fireplaces. With so many kinds of trees I've come to learn something about the burning qualities of various kinds. My favourite is thorn or elm provided the latter has been felled for at least two years. It lasts and does not spit, as do willow or poplar. Indeed, the fastest growing trees are the least useful for firewood, with the possible exception of ash, which will, if split fairly small, burn even when freshly felled. So with alder and chestnut, but beech and birch need to be dried for a year. Oak is best left as long if not longer than elm before being used. I do not care for it, because it needs careful tending, burning best with three or four logs together. There's an old saying — "One log (by itself) won't burn, two logs may burn, three logs will burn and four logs must burn". This applies very much to oak, but for all hardwoods, including birch and alder, which are not very hard, the length of time between felling and burning makes all the difference. One lump of very sere elm will burn by itself once alight, as will most other hardwoods. Oak is one exception, though this did not apply to the oak I used for firewood between 1940 and 1946 at Fordham. This burnt down to a fine brown ash with no problems, and giving plenty of heat if not much flame, having been dead for about 4,000 years. It was bog oak, and hundreds of tons of it were encountered when I was reclaiming land in Burwell Fen.

CHAPTER EIGHTEEN

Uvularia, Veronica . . . .

UNDULATIONS and slopes may be a headache for gardeners in very hilly country, but there's many confined on the flat who must wish for some easy way of breaking up the level. It can of course be superficially achieved by planting suitable trees — especially conifers — so as to avoid uniformity. But to unlevel the soil is a very different matter, as I found out when making my garden. The Dell had a natural appearance, though no more than an elongated depression of about an acre and six to eight feet deep. It was once dug for brick-making clay — probably two centuries ago, and now has a normal topsoil depth of about one foot.

Having made several beds in and around the Dell, with one or two pools, and flint retaining walls, the result was quite pleasing. It was then that I decided to make undulations on an adjoining level piece of similar size. To decide also that sub-soil and top-soil must of necessity lie in correct relation was easy. It was the process of carrying it out that led to the almost frightening upheavals, with raw gorges into the sub-soil in some parts, and great piles of top-soil in others. No matter whether parts were to be lower or higher in level, the top-soil from both had to be moved aside. It was only by adding some sub-soil from where it was to be low on to that due to become higher, that undulations could be achieved, and finished off by replacing the top-soil to both.

Although one could say, when my undertaking was finished, that it had been worthwhile, I would not have tackled it had it not been at a slack time, with tractors available for earthmoving. In smaller gardens earth moving machines cannot be considered, and yet with an open mind ideas can come in which do not involve a big upheaval, nor a vast amount of manual work. Even if a site is dead flat, levels can be broken by skimming off a few inches of soil in one place and adding it to another, and dividing the two by a low wall of brick or stone. The top-soil is often deep enough to allow for such an operation, but if a slight slope already exists, then it becomes much easier to put in one or more low terraces. And if a pool is made, either by a garden feature or for swimming, then the spoil from this can always be utilized, even if clay or chalk, so long as these are added to sub-soil and not placed on top of existing top-soil. Undulations and slopes can add more to a garden than a more pleasing overall appearance. They create different aspects according to which way they face. If both northerly and southerly facing positions are possible, the two distinct ranges of subjects can be grown. Some like all the sun they can get — having come from hotter or drier climes, whilst others revel in cooler conditions. The

The Dell garden at Bressingham.

former generally prefer a well-drained, less rich soil, and the latter a damper, medium soil, with peat or leafmould, and these mostly prefer some shade as well.

Although I am fortunate in having some tall trees as shade providers, their roots, as everyone knows, are often a menace. When these caused losses in my garden I sought ways and means of contriving shady patches well away from trees, and in one spot built a flint retaining wall half way up a north facing slope. The slope was not very great, and the wall was only about three feet high. The first summer revealed that only part of the bed for moisture and shade-loving plants at the foot—about six feet wide—was in shadow. Above the wall, I'd planted a sun-loving variety with too little forethought, for I should have chosen subjects to put immediately inside the top of the wall, which would add a shade contribution. This oversight was easily remedied, and such upstanding subjects as Phormium *tenax* and Miscanthus grass give all the shade needed for those below to grow happily.

Such kinds can be used as shade-providers in any open situation, whether flat or sloping. Phormium *tenax* is evergreen, but has no wide-ranging roots, but one would need to be careful in using evergreen shrubs because generally most of them will have a wider root influence than perennial plants. The same applies to deciduous shrubs, but tall, erect perennials, including tall grasses, will give shade with much less risk of root competition. And if, like Miscanthus or Panicum *virgatum* growth is renewed each year, it will provide the summer shade at only the time of year it is needed. Naturally, as shade providers grow older and larger a wider space needs to be left between them and the subjects they are shading, and it then becomes good practice to thrust a spade deep enough alongside it to curb any encroaching roots. Although they are a garden feature in their own right, they can be so arranged that they fit into the general lay-out of the garden—formal or otherwise. For a damp place—say in the north side of a pool, the "Umbrella Plant" will live up to its name. This is Peltiphyllum *peltatum*. It dies down completely in autumn—when no more shade is needed, and then in spring sends up sprays of small flowers to about two feet. By the time these fade, the leaves are on their way up, opening like flat umbrellas up to 18 inches across and four feet tall. It grows from spreading crowns just below the surface and in time will need curbing by spading back and forking out, if used as a shade-provider for lowlier subjects.

In an earlier book, I described Uvularia *graniflora* as a shade-lover, but a reader from Yorkshire wrote to say that he'd found it much happier in sun. To prove a point, I dug up half my group and planted it in sun. It didn't seem to like it, but since it takes time to become well-established I let it stay for a second season, and as a result had to rescue the few remaining pieces before it vanished entirely. It is a charming plant, carrying pendant lily-type flowers of soft yellow from leafy, 20 inch stems in late spring. As an experiment it had failed. My correspondent no doubt will cling to his belief, just as I reverted to mine. The only point the exercise proved was that it is not safe in all cases to state categorically the best position with regard to sun or shade, nor for that matter the kind of soil a given subject likes best.

This adaptability factor is one which adds to the interest of those who not only go in for a wide variety, but are not afraid to experiment. Experience builds up and the knowledge gained is never forgotten. When growing a subject for the first time one can but take notice of the recorded experience and knowledge of others. I do not hesitate however in saying that Ureospermum *dalechampsii* needs sun, and preferably a southerly slope in well-drained soil. Given this, the flowers, nearly two inches across, of light canary yellow with laminated rayed petals, will continue for most of the summer. The plants are a trifle lax, but not untidily so, for it is no more than twenty inches tall. It flowers so freely that after two or three years it becomes less able to withstand winter, but like other subjects that exhaust themselves in this way, it is easy enough to save some seed for replacement. The many-shaded Centaurea *pulla* and the blood-red Knautia *macedonica* are two others that come to mind in this connection.

There are some plants I cannot keep for long, even though they are reckoned to be fully perennial. Three of them reproduce easily from root cuttings, which should be an indication of having constitutional reserves, but Anchusa *italica* varieties, Catananche, and a few Verbascums seldom survive till spring. Perhaps drainage is not sufficiently sharp, having a clay beneath with a fine but sticky sand lying between it and the top-soil—of which there is no great depth. I have just about given up trying to keep hybrid Verbascums going—'Pink Domino', 'Gainsborough',

'Hartleyi', and the "Cotswold" range, as well as the white 'Mont Blanc', yet the two yellow species V. *thapsiforme* and *chaixii* are fully persistent. I daresay the short-lived V. *phoeniceum* that has been used as a breeding parent for the hybrids with a wider colour range is partially accountable for the weakness, though until I came to Bressingham I had no reason to suspect it.

In the early 1950s I named three Veronicas raised here; 'Barcarolle', 'Minuet' and 'Pavane'. They were selected from a batch of seedlings taken from a pink variety of V. *spicata,* named 'Erica', which had become weakly. V. *spicata* 'incana' was growing nearby, and I was chuffed to find three distinct shades of pink with what appeared to be a very vigorous habit. The lightest pink, 'Minuet', had greyish leaves and graceful, 18-inch spikes, and the deepest, 'Barcarolle', was six inches taller. They were quickly increased and sold quite well, but within a few years they began to lose vigour. 'Pavane' was the first to go—merely through failing to renew basal growth in spring. The others followed, and finally there were none left,

Veronica *spicata* 'minuet', raised at Bressingham.

either on the nursery or in the garden. I missed them, and having given them an initial boost, felt something akin to a guilty conscience in the expectation that plants supplied previously had also died out — especially as both had received Awards of Merit. And then I saw both growing happily in Edinburgh Botanic Gardens, where Alfred Evans told me they had stood and flowered well for several years. I also found them still listed in two retailers' catalogues, and having obtained some plants for old time's sake, found they grew so well that within a year or two they were back in our own catalogue. But I would not be surprised if, because of some fault or lack in the Bressingham soil, they will again show their resentment and languish. I never replaced 'Pavane' to complete the trio, and oddly enough this is the only one of them to be seen in Hilliers catalogue. The blue-flowered 'Saraband', by the way, came from a batch of seedlings from 'Minuet', but this has never looked back.

Violas for bedding were at the height of popularity when I was propagator at R. V. Rogers' nursery, in 1925. He stocked twenty or thirty varieties, but though I framed a thousand or so cuttings of each that autumn, for sale the following spring, double that number was needed of 'Maggie Matt', for which there was always the greatest demand. At that time, and for several years afterwards, there were at least two specialists who grew far larger quantities in a much greater variety, yet now one scarcely ever hears of them, much less sees them. This, no doubt, is another case of over-intensive propagation from cuttings causing vulnerability to disease, especially if they are of hybrid origin. So far as I remember, there was no disease in Michaelmas Daisies fifty years ago, or in Lupins. But now there is, and in the highly-bred 'Russell Lupins' especially it is much safer to rely on seed-raised plants — of which there are strains that will come fairly true to colour.

Much has changed in fifty years, not so much in the pattern of gardening, but with regard to the methods of production and sale of nursery stock. The greatest change has taken place since 1939, as if the War itself was responsible. In many ways it was, for previous to 1939 there was a reasonably stable economy with ample labour at fairly constant rates. There was very little mechanization on nurseries, but competition for outlets was pretty fierce. There were three weekly journals circulating for producers and retailers of nursery stock, along with seeds and sundries, and inside were pages and pages of classified ads. for the whole range. These varied with the seasons, and in spring it was not unusual to see up to fifty offers of Alpine plants and a hundred or more of perennials in the *Horticultural Trade Journal.* By the time this weekly merged with the semi-professional *Gardener's Chronicle*, a few years ago, such advertisements had dwindled to a mere fraction, and now classified ads. occupy but very few pages indeed.

My business had its beginnings, in 1926, in the classified ads. of the *H.T.J.* — offering a few kinds of which I had good stocks at about 25 shillings per hundred, carriage paid for cash with order. That was before I could run to the cost

Part of the nursery — the area of 'Ground Cover' plants, developed since the sons took over.

Michael Warren.

Packing shed at Bloom's Nurseries, Bressingham, during the autumn season. *Michael Warren*

of a printed catalogue—with such a small range to offer not justifying a catalogue anyway.

One tended to imagine that as conditions were, so they would remain. At least, that was what one used to think, and I for one also imagined that war-time inflation would end by about 1950. But since then both change and inflation have gathered momentum, till there are no illusions left on the score of stability. Yet the pattern of gardening has changed to a relatively small extent. Ground-cover has come in and a good deal of labour-demanding, twice-yearly bedding has gone out—except in public parks, the cost of which comes out of the rates. I do not remember seeing, before 1939, any Parks Authority putting up exhibits at the big flower shows. Maybe this was because then the cost would not have been a justifiable charge on the rates, and whether or not it is so nowadays is no business of mine. Nor do I imagine show organizers would query it, for some of the firms who used to stage lavishly-splendid exhibits do so no more, and at the R.H.S. Shows especially there are now to be seen an increasing number from Public Parks and Authorities.

I have always had a somewhat ambivalent attitude towards the R.H.S. Time was when I regarded it with a certain amount of awe. That was when, as a struggling but ambitious young nurseryman, I believed Awards from the R.H.S. must be both advantageous and prestigious. I had much the same respect for its Officers and Council as would a devout churchman for priests and bishops. It was the establishment; the horticultural hierarchy, yet I never yearned or aspired to become a member of its upper crust myself. Indeed, I found that Awards of Merit for plants I'd raised or introduced made little or no difference to sales—or prestige—and I lost respect for it as a body, even when I valued the friendship of individual members.

There were, at least in times past, some nurserymen whose advertisements or printed notepaper tacked F.R.H.S. onto their names, as if this were a hallmark of integrity and respectability. No doubt some of their customers were taken in by it, or it would not have been used in such a way. At that time, anyone could be a Fellow of the R.H.S. for two guineas, which seemed to me so cheap a distinction as to have, in such circumstances, a negative value.

When I learned that the letters V.M.H. stood for the Victoria Medal of Honour, and it was awarded only to make up the constant number of sixty-three holders as death reduced their numbers, it was easier to see them as the élite. As a nurseryman, I could feel somewhat critical of the V.M.H. being awarded, it appeared, mainly to wealthy or titled amateurs, and rarely to those "in trade". Perhaps this was more of an impression than a reality, but it was noticeable that those nurserymen who had been awarded the V.M.H. were those who had rendered service to the R.H.S. itself, rather than to horticulture at large.

It was not until I'd written a book or two and made the new garden that the thought of my being awarded the V.M.H. entered my head. It was planted there by one or two friends and acquaintances who said I deserved it, but far from arousing any hopes or amibitions such remarks brought on cynical thoughts. I felt myself to be a somewhat rebellious loner, having just then resigned from serving on an R.H.S. Committee by way of protest against its rather unwieldly, ineffective procedure. So far as I could see, a V.M.H. would give me little cause for pride, or mean much to anyone else.

It came as quite a surprise, in 1967, to be offered the Veitch Memorial Medal. This ranked as second best to V.M.H., and I guessed it was the first and final gesture by the R.H.S. for any service I'd performed for horticulture. My speciality of hardy plants was not in itself at all high ranking. But as a virtual outsider, very rarely attending R.H.S. meetings, I was not to know that names could be submitted by Fellows to the Council as suggestions for honours which it considered for bestowal. Some of my friends must have been very persistent, for in 1972 I was awarded the V.M.H. as well. As Flora had to remind me, it would please those same friends, and I could not but feel pleased to receive it. Even though I never use the letters after my name and the medal itself has stayed in my study cupboard ever since it was also one-up for hardy perennials.

CHAPTER NINETEEN

Weather, Weed . . . .

WHETHER or not I have any sympathy for those who habitually shrink from manual labour makes no difference. But I cannot help feeling affinity with those who enjoy working, especially where soil and cultivation are concerned. Useful work was held, both by my parents and most of the villagers, as a virtue. There were often times when I felt rebellious, and went off on some carefree and unproductive pursuit — which might turn sour because of a guilty conscience. And then, as I grew nearer to manhood I came to enjoy work and forget any virtuous connection. A love for the soil and of what it would grow did this for me, though some of the jobs I undertook were more out of sheer zest in using my strength to its full capacity.

In the last few years, as I draw nearer to the threshold of old age, I've had to adjust and compromise. My energy no longer keeps pace with my zest for manual work, and I've had to lower my sights when assessing a job, as well as slacken the pace at which I set about it. Whilst accepting increasing limitations on performance, I can still find joy in work. One tends to become craftier with age, applying what wisdom life has taught by scheming out ways of using up less energy in doing a job. There's no sense or wisdom when tackling a job — digging, hoeing or whatever — to go at it all out just because one feels like work after a good night's sleep.

On the nursery, we employ several pensioners, most of whom formerly worked on farms. Until fairly recently it used to irk me to watch their slow progress, whether walking or working, knowing that my own pace was maybe twice as fast. But now that I too am of pensionable age I have to admit they're sensible, for at that pace they can last out the day and accomplish as much or more than if they went too fast to begin with and ran out of steam before the end of the day. As countrymen, theirs is a kind of inbred wisdom, and I fancy townsmen who retire to a place with a garden would find it quite difficult to acquire. They must often have a tussle with themselves — torn between knowing it is good for body and mind to remain active by keeping a garden going, and sitting back idly as life ebbs away. Maybe they lack skill, which includes knowing how to use effort economically, but these are the inseparable twins that will prolong activity and interest in gardening as well as other work.

Percy Piper, who was one of three helpers who stayed on when I took over here had a father, "Old Percy", who also stayed on. In many ways, he was of the same stamp as "Sailor" Smith at Oakington. He enjoyed work, had many skills, and for a few years was the leader of a gang of planters, before this operation was mechanized. Then he became pigman for a time, until age caught up with him, and for several more years he helped part time in the house garden. At nearly eighty he became mole and vermin killer, which involved long walks over the fields. At eighty-six he gave in, but his rood of garden, on which he grew vegetables for sale as well as to eat, was scarcely less productive than before. One day recently I called to see him, and he was digging his neighbour's garden — a man over twenty years his junior.

"Well, you see," Percy explained, "he hasn't got the knack — never been used to it I s'pose, so I do it for him."

"Where there's a will, there's a way" — and I firmly believe it possible, if one has the will, to learn quickly both the skill and the economy of movement necessary for good gardening. If one has retired from some other job there is nothing like gardening to keep up bodily activity and mental serenity and equilibrium. It is a natural activity, and with a determined but receptive mind it can reveal so many of the links that exist between man and nature. Work in a garden can ease worry caused by other stresses in life. This sometimes occurs simply through having some relatively minor worry over an aspect of gardening, or some cultivation problem to solve, that puts the other anxiety into perspective, probably thereby reducing its baneful effect.

To the keen gardener, weather becomes a most important feature in life. The seasons play a more vital part, and one lives closer to nature. One sees that even the worms exposed when digging are also part of nature as are we ourselves. If only we can accept such truths, then we become more in tune, and more integrated.

The soil is not an inanimate substance. It is alive with bacteria and much else that we cannot see, including weed seeds. The roots of trees and plants go searching for their particular needs; the chemical constituents of soil that, when found, produce the qualities and characteristics of each subject. Colours, shapes, seeds, smells, juices, vitamins, proteins and poisons are formed by plants from the soil, by processes we are only just beginning to understand.

Weeds too are part of the natural scheme of things, even if quite rightly, as gardeners, we set out to destroy them. Each kind of weed has its own character, its natural endowment, its means of increase without which it would become extinct. A hoe may sever all but one thread-like root of a weed, and it will still survive, and in such a faculty for survival there could be a message for us, even if our hoeing was faulty and we finish it off. It seems to be a law of nature that, given soil, warmth and moisture, plant growth must take possession. The only true definition of weeds is that they are plants which offend man in his domination over nature, so far as soil is concerned. To us, any plant ranks as a weed if it is a threat or hindrance to what we wish to grow.

To allow weeds to flourish and take over is the greatest disgrace a self-respecting gardener can suffer, and it's a life-long battle to keep them at bay. The saying "One year's seeding means seven years' weeding", is, if anything, an understatement. Weeds will still appear even if a year's seeding is scrupulously prevented, and Charles Darwin is said to have raised over fifty weeds from soil scraped off the feet of a shot pheasant. Getting to know weeds is like getting to know the enemy in a conflict. This includes knowing by what means it exists, persists or increases — whether by seed, or spread, above or below ground. The seed-only method of annuals and monocarpics is the easiest to control, whether by hoe or spray, though the latter should never be used without the utmost discretion.

"Sailor" Smith declared that the best time to kill off annual weeds was before they were large enough to see. By this he meant that hoeing or stirring the soil killed off seedling weeds just as they were germinating. In practical terms, the more immature a crop of weeds the more lethal hoeing is to them, and they have no chance to reproduce. The longer they are left, the longer they will take to die after hoeing, and the more likely they are to rob the soil, as well as drop more seed. If left too long what we wish to grow becomes choked and hand weeding is more likely to be the only remaining remedy. It may well take ten times longer than if the place were hoed a few weeks earlier.

Perennial weeds are a different matter. As small seedlings young dandelions, docks or nettles are as easy to kill as are annuals, but once established some weeds, no matter how they come, will baffle extinction. The worst offenders are those that spread into the roots of plants — as do couch, ground elder, bindweed, sorrel and a few more. But even with these knowing the enemy's habits and being constantly on the watch against infiltration is the surest way of keeping him at bay and harmless. Two of the most dangerously invasive and persistent weeds are bindweed and marestail. Their roots go down so deeply that hoeing is virtually useless and forking out is ineffective. But now these can be treated with a systemic weedkiller. The foliage has to be painted, but though rather a tedious process, it works. My garden has an infestation of mares tail which was there long before the killer was invented, and which cultivation has encouraged. It is already yards across, and has gone beneath the concrete bottom of a pool. There is far too much to paint, and I shrink from the only remedy now open — to take out all the plants and spray the marestail when in full growth. I shrink from tackling what I know eventually must be done because that area will have to be bare of plants for a season.

Not far from a well-known Surrey nursery there lived Gwendoline Anley, another of those ladies devoted to plants, and a generous friend to all who were genuinely interested. She told us, on one of our visits to her, how marestail had come like a curse in her latter days, when being past eighty, she felt unable to combat it. It had spread insidiously, she reckoned, from the nearby nursery, up a hill and into her garden. It had crept beneath paths, hedges and walls till it infested almost the whole of her garden — in which some very choice plants and bulbs and shrubs were growing. And at that time, all she could do was to pull it out from around them, knowing it would reappear within a week or two. Her distress was pathetic, and she died just about the time the only sure killer of marestail was produced.

It is not easy to become philosophical about weeds. In biblical terms they form part of God's curse on Adam for disobedience in the Garden of Eden — a garden in which, presumably, no weeds grew before Adam tasted the forbidden fruit. We can but place weeds on the debit side of gardening, along with inclement weather — drought, frost, excessive wet and tearing winds — and the pests and diseases. We can combat some of these, but some that can't be cured must be endured. Weariness of body and vexation of mind are part of the gardener's lot in life; and yet there are compensations. If we never became weary, there would be no refreshment in sleep, nor would we experience the joyful relief of a much-needed rain or the peace after a gale has subsided. And if there were no weeds — could there, I wonder, be any deeper satisfaction in cultivating? To be free of them, if only temporarily, by our own efforts, is not without its reward, and this can be accepted as such if we regard them as part of the wide, intricate spectrum of nature.

It is also part of the natural order of things that we should use our brains as well as our bodies. It is up to us to supplement physical effort with skill and craftiness; to pull a fast one over nature whenever we can get away with it. This is what gardening is all about, so long as we don't forget that nature holds a good many trump cards, one of which is the ace of scythes.

CHAPTER TWENTY

Youth, Zest . . . .

YOUTH is mostly the powerhouse of ambition, and in the process both impatience and intolerance can also be generated, especially for elders who appear to stand in the way. There was certainly a time when I felt like that about my own father. I did not think of him as being a tolerant man, though he undoubtedly was. The period when I chafed was brief, partly because my bent in horticulture differed from his, but chiefly because he gave me the opportunity of becoming my own master by moving to Mildenhall when I was twenty-four.

When Robert, the eldest of my two sons, was that age, he had spent several years away from home and was by no means sure he wanted to return. He had sampled nursery work at home on leaving school, but after a few months decided that farming was more to his liking. Beginning as a pupil, he worked on four different farms, but drifted into dairy farming because of the better prospects this offered for a responsible job. But after a time he found that being in charge of a dairy herd in Northamptonshire was a dead-end job, and that after all, there was a future for him at Bressingham on the farming side.

At about the same time, in 1964 Adrian also returned from his wanderings, having worked on a variety of jobs in the U.S.A., and gained nursery experience in Denmark and Switzerland. Both boys were ambitious. The question did not arise at that time as to wehn they would take over from me, because they still had much to learn. With Robert twenty-five and Adrian twenty-four, it was obvious not only that both were setting their sights at taking over, but that they were planning to expand when that time came. For the next few years it was tricky. I had no wish to be repressive, and no intention either of holding on to the reins for any longer than was necessary. I was fifty-eight at the time, and had thought sixty-five was about the right age to hand over.

But it had to come gradually. Robert was virtually in charge of the farm and machinery by 1964, and Adrian had expressed the wish to go in for dwarf Conifers and Heathers as his own special department. I could do no other than agree, remembering my own urges went well outside my father's footsteps. But I kept control from the centre. Whilst giving in whenever I could agree to their suggestions and requests for changes and improvements, I still signed all the cheques and opened the mail. They may well have chafed because of this, but I saw these two responsibilities as the remaining bastions in the control of a business I'd begun almost from scratch in 1931. But now, with over 100 helpers on the staff I wanted to be sure that when I gave up these vital duties, they would be in safe hands.

But it had to come—and they became joint Managing Directors before I was sixty-five. About time too, they may have thought, but from the time they signed the cheques and opened the mail, I could but become a figure-head in practice, though Chairman in title. Naturally they referred any important issues to me, and though I had the power of veto, I had no wish to use it. It would have cramped their initiative and disheartened them had I done so just because their ideas of progress were different from mine.

The firm's directors (Blooms Nurseries Ltd) 1973. Left to right: Adrian Bloom, Mary Fox (Secretary), Lawrence Fleetwood, Alan Bloom, Maurice Prichard, Flora Bloom (Author's wife), Robert Bloom (eldest son). *Michael Warren.*

Since then the business has forged ahead—a little too fast for my liking, till I reminded myself of my own ideas and outlook at their age. I could also remind myself that, but for them, I would have begun to cut back on production at about the time they took over. The nurseryman's life is very exacting and having made a large garden and acquired a number of steam engines, with ideas taking shape for a live steam museum it would have been too much to keep up the nursery as well, at the size to which it had grown by 1970.

Between them, Robert and Adrian have some real achievements to their credit. They are less inhibited about capital investment than I—shortage of capital over a lifetime made me a skimper, going mostly for the cheapest rather than the best, to make do rather than launch out on such things as machinery, buildings and equipment. New offices and packing shed came quickly after they took over, and acres of polythene houses went up, as production of conifers, heathers and ground cover plants expanded. Processes were streamlined and mechanized wherever possible, training programmes inaugurated, and in every direction expansion became evident. On Adrian's initiative a consortium was formed of five East Anglian wholesale producers, known as the Anglia Group, so as to dovetail selling and deliveries to their mutual advantage.

My own inclinations would have been to carry on, as I'd done for forty years, with perennials and alpines in the widest possible variety. Already ours was the largest nursery of its type in Europe, but I tended to shut my eyes to changes taking place. Retailers we had supplied were having to meet a demand for pre-packed and container-grown plants, and I had no enthusiasm for the extra trouble this meant for us as wholesale producers. There was also a demand for ground-covering subjects, and on principle I disliked it. If people were encouraged to lay down ground coverers it was likely to deter them from growing the choicer kinds. To me "ground cover" was a retrogressive form of gardening and I saw no good reason for pandering to it.

But Robert and Adrian were more realistic. They believed that if new trends in sales existed, then they must be catered for. Already Adrian's conifers and heathers were taking on, and new techniques were beginning to have their effect on production generally. Although I saw much less of the nursery, as a matter both of policy, and because I had full-time job in the garden and on the steam venture, occasional visits to the nursery brought shocks of one kind or another. To see frames full of Hypericum *calycinum* (Rose of Sharon) cuttings, acres of Bergenias, and vast quantities of heathers, conifers and even common Ivy, amongst the ground-covering plants, brought home the magnitude, not only of the changes, but of the rate of expansion. When I counselled Adrian to go easy on expansion, he'd grin and assure me I had no need to worry. Maybe this was the case, and sales were undoubtedly on the up and up. Undoubtedly, too, both he and Robert were on the ball, and were probably making a closer study of profitability than I ever did.

The fears which I held of economic difficulties to come were borne out in 1974. It was mainly because of this that I advised cautious expansion, to avoid the headaches I'd known so keenly, so often, of being financially overstretched. But when galloping inflation hit us severely in 1974-5 I hadn't the heart to rub it in, knowing that had I been in their shoes I too would have gone all out for expansion.

Once or twice a year I take just a few days off to visit gardens and nurseries where the chance of a swop between friends exists. On one such trip, late in 1973, I visited Old Court Nurseries, near Malvern, after an interval of a dozen years. Percy Picton, the owner, was at one end of a glasshouse as I entered the other.

"Hullo, stranger", he called. And then over the handshake, he gave me a quizzical look, and said, "I hear Bressingham is no longer a nursery. You've turned it into a plant factory by all accounts".

Of course I hastened to absolve myself. Percy Picton is one of the most knowledgeable of plantsmen and has many a rare treasure on a quite small nursery, and I wanted to assure him that my own interest had not waned.

There was a period of two or three years when, to some of my gardening friends, my interest in plants appeared to be secondary. That was when my steam engine hobby erupted into a live steam museum. It was the enthusiasm shown by visitors to the garden which sparked it off, making me realize that here there was the scope and an opportunity so unique that I could not resist it. I had to be the kingpin in such a development and for a time my thoughts and energies were divided. But only for a time. I was never in doubt that once the museum was organised with a competent staff, then plants would again take first place. It was not a case of desertion for a new love, but if the occasional remarks and innuendos from those who did not understand were rather hurtful, for some time now nine-tenths of my time has been spent with plants.

Now that the steam museum, with over forty engines of many types, has become established — as the most comprehensive live museum in Britain — I realize that both this and the garden will need constant supervision. Both grew as a result of my own enthusiasm, with no thought at the outset of the extent to which they would develop. Unlike the nursery business, neither were the result of a clear cut, long term ambition, at least not until they were well under way, as I realised the full scope and potential at my door, awaiting completion. Both are my personal ventures, especially as past endeavours in building up the nursery business and farming activities are no longer solely in my hands. The steam museum could continue without my personal supervision, since it has become a Charitable Trust having some historical importance.

But just as I now find more joy than ever in the garden and its plants, so I realize that it is the most vulnerable of my interests, if for any reason it becomes neglected. If I could consider myself as being indispensible anywhere this is the place. But the time must come, and it is but wishful thinking to imagine that the garden will be carried on exactly as I would have it myself. Whoever it is who eventually follows me will have their own ideas and ways of working. I may leave ample notes and instructions to a future curator, but this will not ensure that they are used. The hundred and one seasonal jobs I now undertake or supervise, the details of knowing what to do, when and how to do it, are only part of the process of keeping the garden with its 5,000 kinds up to scratch. There is also the necessity of knowing where every kind is placed; of labelling, of making changes of position where and when necessary; of spotting possible improvements and keeping up swops and the intake of newcomers. There is scope for more hybridising; for working up stocks of rare or unusual kinds worthy of wider distribution, to say nothing of experimenting so as to widen the knowledge of plant behaviour under varying conditions.

Author taking a special party by train round the nursery.

'Grognedil' with passengers on an open day pauses (or poses) on the two mile Nursery Railway.

Michael Warren

I seem to be as far from being satisfied with my garden now as when I was in the process of making it. Perfection is elusive, rather like a will o' the wisp. During the summer I make page after page of notes as each bed is examined, not only to record jobs I consider necessary when planting time comes again, but where improvements in grouping of layout could be made. By the following spring these notes are ticked off as having been done, and yet within weeks I see other faults, calling for another round of note-taking. I fancy this is as it should be. It is good to aim for perfection, even with the realization that it will never be attained. If it were, if the time came when there was nothing needing to be done, then gardening would lose its stimulus and interest.

I have been dubbed as a leading authority on hardy perennials. Seeing such remarks in print tends to make me wince inwardly, for having learned something, I realize it is a mere fraction of what still remains outside my knowledge. One can be philosophical about this. Any knowledge gained is worth putting on record, because someone, sometime may be able to make use of it. In a wider sense it is as much a contribution to posterity as leaving a garden such as mine in the hope or expectation that it will be permanently maintained. A private garden, developed and maintained during one person's life can become a wilderness within a few months if no provision is made. I have seen a few such once famous gardens—such as Lissadell in County Sligo—and the sight is pitiful.

Zest, I suppose is the greatest gift a gardener can possess. At any rate gardening must be a bind to those who can find no zest for it. It can scarcely be acquired by sheer will power, for that would make it into a kind of penance. But it has been known for men, especially, who have taken on a simple gardening chore as a duty, to become more deeply involved through their interest being aroused. A spark may be kindled—given an open, receptive mind—by some quite casual observation, something about a flower, or whatever, he had never noticed before.

As with most conversions on the emotional level in other aspects of life it is when a first glimmer is followed up that the stimulus grows till it develops into zeal or zest. I can think of several examples of people who did not take to gardening until they reached middle age, and one or two who began when they retired from business or a profession. Some became famous in their particular field. For women, gardening zest seems to come more easily, though perhaps I am basing this generalization on an impression rather than fact. The fact is, of course, that zest for gardening—a love of plants and flowers which goes beyond mere visual appeal—is spread without regard to sex. It is kindled and sustained without regard to age. Those who possess it do not lose it, even when too old or infirm to practise it, for the mind and heart often keep going when the body has to give in. Zest springs from within, and I fancy that those who possess zest for gardening are most likely to follow it actively into a ripe old age.

One must however be realistic, and avoid becoming sentimental or maudlin. With two sons and three grandsons, as well as three daughters I can feel hopeful. I can also be thankful that I am still able to enjoy work, including manual jobs which I could, if I chose, tell others to do. I like to think that this is one of the secrets of living fully—to use physical as well as mental energy on some worthwhile project that keeps us in touch with, and in tune with nature. As humans we are, whether we like it or not, part of the natural order of Life, and the basis of all Life is Mother Earth.

Index

Alan Bloom.

Michael Warren